# BLOGGIN' BASEBALL

# (from the bench)

Copyright © 2013 Andrew Wolfenson

ISBN-13: 978-0615780856

ISBN-10: 0615780857

**Balding Legal Publishing**

**2414 Morris Avenue, Suite 104, Union, NJ 07083**

## FOREWARD

*"When I think of Andrew Wolfenson, two things come to mind: 'He's a schmuck!' (coincidentally, my reflex reaction to most Yankee fans) and 'He's a mensch!' (my reflex reaction to only a select few of the people I've known since childhood).*

*As it relates to Bloggin' Baseball, his 'mensch-i-ness' far surpasses his 'schmuck-i-ness' and I'm proud to say that 'I knew him when.'*

*Andrew's love and respect for our national pastime shine through from first pitch to final out. His 'extra innings' are especially insightful and make for perfect post-scripts.*

*Written with equal measures of passion, wit, and acerbic humor (See, eSpecially, hi\$ 5th inning Bo\$ton Red \$ox entry), Wolfenson more than capably lives up to his self-proclaimed billings of 'Oracle,' 'Seer,' and 'Know-it-All.'*

*In this fan's opinion, Bloggin' Baseball makes for an All-Star addition to anyone's reading list."*

*- Marc Ernay, Morning Sports Anchor, New York City News Radio Station*

In 1988, I graduated from Franklin & Marshall College and officially abandoned any hopes of earning a living as a sportswriter. I had spent a large part of the prior three years in the office of my college newspaper, progressing from contributing writer to Sports Editor to Editor-in-Chief. The fact that an Accounting major was in charge of the newspaper ruffled the feathers of some in the English department, but that did not stop me from spending what I believed was a successful year at its helm. The cover photo (well, the head in the cover photo) was actually taken in the newspaper office somewhere between 1986 and 1988.

A career in the law, however, promised to be a better way to make a living and support a future family, so I decided to enroll in law school upon graduation. Gone were the hopes of sportswriting, replaced with visions of representing athletes and becoming a sports agent. That never materialized, but I returned to New Jersey (having gone to Fordham Law School in New York) and have practiced law in the Garden State since that time.

A wife, three children, and a dog later, the desire to write still remained. I had tried to write a novel in 1994, but was unable to find an agent and placed the manuscript to the side – but am now re-writing it and hope to have it published in the near future. In what will seem like a pattern, it concerned sports – a fantasy baseball league.

Years later, the internet offered new possibilities. In 2009, I joined the blogosphere and began to write about a myriad of topics – but the most frequent topic was baseball. Many of those posts concerned the New York Yankees, the team for which I have unabashedly rooted for four decades.

Some posts went fairly unnoticed, but numerous offerings earned me the designation of "Editor's Pick," and, more importantly, landed me on the blog's front page – and which led to increased readership for those posts, some of which drew in excess of several thousand readers apiece. I hit real paydirt with a pair of posts about Joe Paterno's fall from grace, both of which still stand as my most-viewed posts ever.

It has been suggested to me that I should put some of the old posts into book form, so that they could be read together. Hence this project – included in this book you will find over forty of my posts from the various sites, grouped into nine "innings" by their respective subject matters. All of them have been changed from their original forms, sometimes to correct information, and other times to correct (gasp) typographical errors. I have also added "extra innings" to most, additional commentary about the subject matter to either clarify or update the subject matter therein. I hope you enjoy, even if you do not agree with the posts or my conclusions. The ability to disagree about teams, players, and perspectives is what makes following sports so great.

## ACKNOWLEDGEMENTS

In keeping with the baseball theme of this book, I would like to thank the veritable All-Star team of people who have helped with its completion.

The team's "public relations department" – first, the creator of the book cover – as with *In His Own Defense,* Diana Ani Stokely has brilliantly created a perfect visual manifestation of my writing. Also, Brian Lewbart, whose photo of the 1987-88 *College Reporter* Editor-in-Chief served as the cover's foundation, and Marc Ernay, for the overly-kind words contained above in the Foreward.

I may seem like a narcissist, but I am going to name myself the starting pitcher for the team – I did *write* the book. My catcher is the person who often calls the shots for me and who serves as my battery mate in life – my wife, Jennifer. My amazing trio of daughters will be the infielders – in age order, Sara (first base), Danielle (second base), and Alina (third base). My four-legged son will play shortstop, the position that his namesake has manned for almost two decades as a member of the Yankees.

The outfield is manned by a three friends (and, ardent Yankees' fans) who have provided invaluable support, inspiration, and feedback for many of the blogs contained in this book – in alphabetical order, George Fiszer (left field), Jon Schaechter (center field), and Mike Weinreich (right field).

Serving as joint designated hitters are the people who served as Editors for the book - my parents, Gil and Debby Wolfenson; it took me a long time, but finally, I was able to find a productive use for their need to nag at and correct my mistakes. Their 47 years of practice made it any easy task, no doubt, and it seemed only fitting to have them serve as editors because any writing ability that I may possess is inherited from them.

And lest there be any doubt, I would take this All-Star team over any of the teams included in Chapter Seven, without question.

# TABLE OF CONTENTS

## Fifth Inning:  OTHER YANKEE-RELATED BLOGS

## Sixth Inning:  THE METS AND THEIR POOR FANS

# FIRST INNING

## TRIBUTES

Most people think that the word "blog" equates to "rant", and that all blogs are simply written versions of the writer's tantrum. Sometimes, this is true, as some of the later chapters in this book will prove. There are times, however, when the purpose of the blog is to educate, to inform, and to provide information that might not otherwise be available to the reader.

It is also said that it is possible to recognize a person in their writings. That may be the case here. This chapter contains five posts, which I believe are reflective of my background and personality. The first tells the story of Hank Greenberg, and celebrates what would have been his 100th birthday on January 1, 2011. The second (correctly) predicts an MVP win for Ryan Braun in 2011, the latest on a very short list of Jewish Most Valuable Player winners, and discusses the possibility of an Israeli team participating in the World Baseball Classic. Both posts celebrate, as much as possible, the pride in my religion as exhibited by so few players.

Two Yankee-related posts are also included. First, the retirement of Andy Pettitte, at which time I lamented the end of the recent run of Yankee "Glory Years" – although Pettitte later returned to the mound. The second is a brief ode to the owner of the Yankees, written in the minutes after I learned of his death.

Lastly, you will find my eulogy for Gary Carter, a man who played with unbridled enthusiasm and joy even when surrounded by a team comprised, in part, of drug users and addicts. It is a perfect segue into the next chapter.

# Happy 100th Birthday, Hank Greenberg (December 30, 2010)

New Year's Day is a time of new beginnings, as we anxiously greet a fresh twelve months full of hope and promise. It is a time for us to look back on the year gone by, of triumphs and sorrows, and a day for us to remember the recently departed. We remember those whom we knew personally, those who somehow touched or enriched our lives.

We also recall public figures who perished during the year, whether statesmen, celebrities, or athletes. And on the first day of January, 2011, there is one other person whom we should all remember, a man who died almost a quarter century ago but whose contributions to his people, religion and country were unmatched. That person was Hank Greenberg.

Hank Greenberg would have been 100 years old this New Year's Day.

In a major league career that spanned 17 years but which was interrupted by military service, Greenberg compiled a .313 lifetime batting average while hitting 331 homers with 1,276 RBI. Twice the American League's Most Valuable Player (1935, 1940), he set major league records for home runs (58) and runs batted in (183) in a season by a right-handed hitter. He led the American League in homers four times, in RBI's four times, and doubles three times. And he amassed these statistics even though he missed almost four full seasons, in the prime of his career, to fight for the United States in World War II.

Most importantly, Hank Greenberg emerged as one of baseball's premier first basemen (along with Lou Gehrig and Jimmy Foxx) in the 1930's, carried his Detroit Tigers teammates to postseason success, and did so while carrying the unenviable burden of being the pre-eminent Jewish baseball player of his time.

12

In fact, Greenberg remains the greatest Jewish player ever. He and Sandy Koufax, unarguably the greatest Jewish pitcher, are two of only three Jewish players enshrined in the Baseball Hall of Fame. No Jew has approached Greenberg's career statistics, and none of those who followed in his footsteps have been forced to endure the anti-Semitism and bigotry that so insidiously attempted to thwart his accomplishments.

Seeing me reading *"The Story of My Life"*, Greenberg's autobiography, my mother told me how proud my grandfather and his friends were of Greenberg when he played, and about how they all looked up to and related to him based on his religion. On the baseball diamond, he was the best Jew that the game had ever seen up, and he blasted open the doors for those Jewish stars who followed after him, including Koufax, Al Rosen, and others.

Raised in an Orthodox Jewish household, it appears that, with the exception of not playing one Yom Kippur (after he famously stroked two home runs on Rosh Hashanah after receiving a Rabbi's blessing to play), he did not publicly practice the religion as an adult. Although by most counts he was not outwardly religious during his playing days, however, it is clear that Greenberg felt the pressure of his religion:

*"Being Jewish did carry with it a special responsibility. After all, I was representing a couple of million Jews among a hundred million Gentiles, and I was always in the spotlight ... I was there every day, and if I had a bad day, every son of a bitch was calling me names so that I had to make good. I just had to show them that a Jew could play ball." (1)*

According to those who played with Greenberg, the vitriol came from fans and other players alike. As stated by his former teammate, Birdie Tebbetts, *"There was nobody in the history of the league who took more abuse than Greenberg, unless it was Jackie Robinson ... I was with Hank when it was*

13

*happening and I heard it. However, Hank was not only equal to it, he was superior to most of the people who were yelling at him ... Hank consistently took more abuse than anyone I have ever known ... Nobody else could have withstood the foul invectives that were directed toward Greenberg ..." (2)*

A similar analogy between Greenberg and Jackie Robinson, the first African-American to play in the major leagues, was drawn by Al Rosen, himself a Jew and one of the great players of the 1950's:

*"Remember, Greenberg was to Jewish ballplayers what Jackie Robinson was to blacks. I'm not trying to draw an analogy between the problems the blacks have and the Jews, but there were problems nevertheless. Whenever people don't come to grips with that there can be a real problem. And Greenberg went through a great deal and he paved the way for people like me." (3)*

Greenberg himself noted the similarities between their respective situations: *"The more they ride him [Robinson] the more they will spur him on. It threw me a lot when I first came up. I know how he feels." (4)*

Ken Burns, who produced the epic *"Baseball"* video series for PBS almost two decades ago, noted that due to prejudices many of the Jewish players before Greenberg had changed their names, but that Greenberg "had never even considered doing" so. (5)

His heroics, however, were not reserved for the ball field. He was the first star player to enlist following the attack on Pearl Harbor, and, along with players like Ted Williams, Bob Feller, and Joe DiMaggio, spent what could have been the peak years of their careers fighting for our country. In fact, he had been drafted previously, but his term of service had ended and he was released by the Army on December 5, 1941. The bombing of Pearl Harbor took place two days later, and Greenberg, selflessly, immediately re-enlisted, noting that *"[w]e are in trouble, and there is only one thing for me to do - return to the service ...*

14

*this doubtless means I am finished with baseball ... But all of us are confronted with a terrible task - the defense of our country and the fight for our lives." (6)*

He did return to baseball after the war, played two more years with the Tigers, and then spent the last year of his career playing for the Pittsburgh Pirates. He then held ownership interests and front-office positions with the Cleveland Indians and later the Chicago White Sox, becoming one of baseball's first Jewish team owners and again facing anti-Semitism as he blazed a trail for others to follow. Following his stints as a baseball executive, he co-founded a successful investment firm, eventually retired, and died of cancer in 1986.

Hank Greenberg would have turned 100 years old on New Year's Day. He should be remembered, especially now, as an outstanding ballplayer, as a patriot and decorated war veteran, and a successful executive and businessman. His accomplishments on the field, in many categories, stand second only to the great Lou Gehrig among American League first basemen of the 1930's and 1940's. He selflessly gave up four years of his career to fight in World War II, and it is unheard of (with the exception of the late Pat Tillman) to think that an athlete, in the prime of his career, would voluntarily leave the game and fight in a war. Others did it then, but he was the first.

And most importantly, he should be remembered for his religious pride, for standing up to the anti-Semitism that followed his every step on the ball field. Like Jackie Robinson, he withstood the pressures of being different, shouldered the rampant bigotry and cries of hatred, and he proved that a person's religion, like the color of one's skin, did not preclude him from becoming one of the game's elite.

Happy Birthday, Hank. And thank you.

Citations:

(1) The Story of My Life, Hank Greenberg with Ira Berkow, 1989, at pp. 110-11.

(2) Id. at p. 98.

(3) Id. at p. 212.

(4) Id. at p. 181.

(5) Baseball: an Illustrated History, Geoffrey C. Ward and Ken Burns, 1994, at p. 249.

(6) Id. at pp. 275-76.

**Extra innings:** After I penned this blog, I had the pleasure of watching "The Life and Times of Hank Greenberg", a documentary produced in 1998. The winner of numerous "best documentary" awards, it is a must-see not only for Jews, but for all baseball fans.

I forgot to include in the original post that in 1999, he ranked as # 37 on *The Sporting News'* list of 100 Greatest Baseball Players. He was also nominated as a finalist for the MLB All-Century team. Lou Gehrig, not surprisingly, garnered the most votes of any first baseman. The second leading vote-getter was Mark McGwire, fresh off his synthetically-enhanced record-breaking 1998 campaign. If the vote were taken today, no doubt the results would be much different.

# Jews, Israel and Baseball - A *Shidduch*? (November 21, 2011)

Tomorrow, Ryan Braun of the Milwaukee Brewers may be announced as the winner of the 2011 National League Most Valuable Player award. If so, he will be the first Jewish player to be showered with shouts of *"mazel tov"* for capturing the MVP award since 1963. This comes at a time when published reports indicate that three former Jewish major leaguers have thrown their support behind Israel's bid to host the 2013 World Baseball Classic. The concept of a Jew being named MVP for the first time in almost half a century and the Jewish homeland being selected to host a world baseball tournament is staggering. While it is unlikely that the Classic will be awarded to the always-volatile country, the mere fact that it is being considered, along with the successes being achieved by Braun and other current Jewish ballplayers, signals the beginning of a new era in Jewish baseball.

Up until this point, one would have been hard-pressed to term baseball a "Jewish" sport. Only three Jewish-born players are enshrined in the Baseball Hall of Fame, and only four Jews have won Most Valuable Player awards. The 1930's through 1950's, a time when most Jews lived in the country's major cities and played "ghetto-friendly" games like basketball, created an era of Jewish basketball all-stars and boxing champions, but few baseballers. Now, a trio of current superstars – Braun, Boston's Kevin Youkilis, and Texas' Ian Kinsler, has established this as the most prolific generation of major league baseball ballplayers.

Hank Greenberg was the first Jewish superstar in the major leagues, and the man known as "Hammerin' Hank" (prior to future home run king Hank Aaron) paved the way for future Jewish players much like Jackie Robinson later did for African-American ballplayers. Despite enduring rampant anti-Semitism and missing four years while serving in World War II, Greenberg, a hulking first baseman, compiled a .313 lifetime batting average to complement his 331 home runs and 1,276 RBIs. He won the American League's Most Valuable Player award twice, in 1935 and 1940, and set major league records for both home runs (58) and RBIs (183) by a right-hand hitter. Also, although he played first base at the same time as Yankee legend Lou Gehrig, he was still selected to play in five All-Star games. Following his retirement, he held ownership interests and front-office positions with the Cleveland Indians and Chicago White Sox. He was elected to the Hall of Fame in 1956, the first Jew so enshrined.

Most importantly, however, Greenberg, a true *mensch*, withstood the vitriolic comments and insults being hurled at him by anti-Semitic opponents and fans. Greenberg's heroics blazed a difficult trail to follow, but two members of the 1940's-1950's Cleveland Indians attempted to take the mantel from him. During a fifteen-year career, Lou Boudreau won the 1944 batting championship and, while a player-manager for the Indians, captured the 1948 American League Most Valuable Player award. He also served as the radio voice for the Chicago Cubs for several decades, and was inducted into the Hall of Fame in 1970. His teammate, Al Rosen, was one of the standouts on the 1954 championship-winning Indians, a four-time All-Star, and won the 1953 MVP award. Rosen later served in front-office positions with the Indians and the New York Yankees, his stint with the Yankees taking place during the team's "Bronx Zoo" successes of the late 1970's.

The greatest of all Jewish players, however, was Sandy Koufax. Arguably the best left-hander ever to pitch in the majors and on everyone's short list for best pitchers of all-time, the Brooklyn-born Koufax simply dominated the National League from 1961 through 1966. In the four seasons from 1963 through his retirement in 1966, he posted three seasons of sub-2.00 ERA's (leading the National League in ERA each season) and led the National League in wins three times. In fact, in 1963, 1965, and 1966, he led the league in wins, ERA, and strikeouts, capturing pitching's equivalent of the "Triple Crown." (as a side note, his totals in each of those years would have led the American League as well, further evidencing his dominance over baseball during that period) He pitched four no-hitters, including a perfect game, was selected as the

Cy Young Award winner (there was only one for both leagues) in 1963, 1965, and 1966, and captured the NL MVP award in 1963, the last Jew to do so. Retiring at age 30 after only twelve seasons (ten full) due to recurring arm troubles, he was elected to the Hall of Fame in 1972. He was also the only Jew selected by the fans to Major League Baseball's all-time team in 1999.

Koufax also made the legendary decision not to pitch Game One of the 1965 World Series because it fell on the Jewish Day of Atonement, Yom Kippur. The Dodgers' other superstar pitcher, Don Drysdale, took the mound for Los Angeles that day and did not pitch well, giving up seven runs in less than three innings. When manager Walt Alston came to the mound to replace him during the game, Drysdale remarked "I bet right now you wish I was Jewish, too." In 1934, it should be noted, Greenberg also refused to play on Yom Kippur. He did, however, play on Rosh Hashanah, the Jewish New Year, receiving a Rabbi's blessing to play and slamming two home runs.

Those four players formed the veritable "Mount Rushmore" of Jewish ballplayers until the current era. There were other successes - Ken Holtzman was a key member of the 1970's Oakland A's champions (along with fellow Jew Mike Epstein) and threw two no-hitters during his career. Orioles' pitcher Steve Stone captured the AL Cy Young Award in 1980. Other Jews were notable for various reasons, such as World War II spy Moe Berg and Ron Blomberg, who famously served as the first Designated Hitter in baseball history and, in recent years, has managed a team in the Israeli baseball league. History is also replete with Jewish owners and front-office leaders, including current commissioner and former Brewer owner Bud Selig and a quartet of *machers* who now preside as their team's General Managers: Ruben Amaro, Jr. (Philadelphia), Jon Daniels (Texas), Theo Epstein (Chicago Cubs), and Andrew Friedman (Tampa Bay).

The three former players who are now supporting Israel's bid for the World Baseball Classic are Brad Ausmus, Gabe Kapler, and Shawn Green. A catcher who spent the majority of his career with Houston, Ausmus won three

Gold Glove awards, was selected to the All-Star game in 1999, and stroked over 1,500 hits over his 18 big-league seasons. Kapler, who was once considered to be one of baseball's best prospects and was nicknamed the "Hebrew Hammer", toiled for six teams over a twelve-year career. Sporting various tattoos, including a Star of David tattoo on his left calf and a Holocaust-inspired tattoo on his right, his career was an unfortunate example of unfulfilled potential; despite his "success" being *bashert*, according to scouts, his career amounted to little more than *bupkes*. He did, however, enjoy some *n*aches and celebrated as a member of the 2004 Red Sox championship team.

The best of these three is unquestionably Green. Over a fourteen-year career spent primarily with Toronto and the Los Angeles Dodgers, Green slammed 328 home runs, hit 445 doubles, and knocked in 1,070 runs. His 49 home runs in 2001 are the most ever by a Dodgers' player, and he exceeded 40 homers in a season three times. A two-time All-Star, he also won both the Gold Glove and "Silver Slugger" awards in 1999.

The current crop of major leaguers, including the three All-Stars noted above, are the best group ever to be playing at one time. In his five seasons, Braun has already stroked 161 home runs and amassed 531 RBI's to go along with his .312 batting average. Widely recognized as one of baseball's premier players, for each of the last four years he has been selected to the All-Star game and has been awarded baseball's "Silver Slugger" award, given annually to the best hitters at each position. Youkilis was a key member of the Red Sox 2007 championship team, has been a three-time All-Star, and 2007 Gold Glove winner. Kinsler, along with fellow Jew Scott Feldman, has been a key member of the Rangers' team that advanced to the World Series in each of the past two years, and was selected to the All-Star game in 2008 and 2010.

And there are other notable Jewish players – Mets' first baseman Ike Davis (his mother is Jewish) and Tampa Bay outfielder Sam Fuld are stars in the making, and Arizona pitcher Jason Marquis has won over 100 major league games.

Israel is one of 16 teams which has been invited to play in next year's World Baseball Classic qualifying round, and the top four teams from that competition will advance to the 2013 WBC tournament. According to Israeli baseball officials, the Israeli team, if it were to qualify for the WBC, would seek to recruit Jewish professionals to play for the team. Green has also indicated his desire to again put on a uniform and play if asked, meaning that the Israeli team could possibly be set up as follows:

1B Ike Davis

2B Ian Kinsler

SS Danny Valencia (Twins' 3B would move to SS)

3B Kevin Youkilis

OF Ryan Braun

OF Sam Fuld

OF Shawn Green

C Brad Ausmus (42 and retired since 2009, but the best option)

P Jason Marquis/Scott Feldman

With the exception of the aged catcher, this would be a pretty formidable line-up. This *minyan* could contend with the Latin powerhouse teams of Venezuela and the Dominican Republic and, with a little bit of *mazel*, could unseat the two-time defending champs, Japan. If nothing else, a good showing by the team will allow Jews over the world to *kvell* over its accomplishments, and could go a long way toward erasing the stigma against Jews' inability to excel in sports, as was so memorably stated in the movie "Airplane." The heroics of the current crop of Jewish all-stars, I would urge, is certainly sufficient to fill much more than a light-reading leaflet.

## _Yiddish/Hebrew Glossary (in order of their appearance above)_

_Shidduch_ – match, as in matchmaking

_Mazel tov_ – congratulations / good luck

_Mensch_ – upstanding citizen / a person of integrity

_Machers_ – important people

_Bashert_ - predestined

_Bupkes_ – literal translation is "beans" but figuratively means "nothing"

_Minyan_ – group of ten (usually men) needed for a proper prayer group

_Mazel_ - luck

_Kvell_ – to feel happy and proud

**Extra Innings:  Ryan Braun did capture the MVP award in 2011, and then followed up his success with a stellar 2012 campaign after which he finished second in that year's MVP voting. He did this in spite of allegations regarding PED usage (see Second Inning).**

**Brad Ausmus managed the Israeli squad in the qualifying games for the 2013 World Baseball Classic, and the roster included Shawn Green as an outfielder. The team, however, failed to qualify for the tournament.**

**In 2013, the Yankees signed Kevin Youkilis to play third base, in place of the injured Alex Rodriguez. In the past, the trading of a Jewish player to a New York team would have led to a great deal of media coverage about the player and his effect on the local Jewish community, as was the case with Shawn Green when he was playing for the New York Mets. In this case, however, the religious angle of his signing has been minimal at best. Perhaps that is due to the fact that Youkilis gained his greatest fame as a member of the hated Red Sox and his prior battles with New York pitcher Joba Chamberlain provided better fodder for the newspapers.**

In the initial version, I had also included a paragraph about Rod Carew, or, as he was referred to by Adam Sandler, "Hall of Famer Rod Carew". It was pointed out to me, however, that Rod Carew never actually converted to Judaism. His wife was Jewish, but the stories of him having converted were apparently false. His success on the diamond did lead to one piece of trivia regarding his Jewish-or-non-Jewish status, however – in 1979, for the first and only time in Major League history, the batting champions of both the American and National League wore "Star of David" necklaces around their necks. Carew won the AL batting title that year, and wore his necklace, presumably, in honor of his wife's religion even though he had not converted. The NL winner was Dave Parker of the Pirates, who wore the necklace because, as he explained, "my name is David and I am a star."

I had the good fortune to meet Rod Carew at an autograph show in Secaucus, NJ. He was, possibly, the nicest man you could ever meet. While other former players begrudgingly took photos with the fans who had turned out (and paid) to obtain their signatures, when I asked Carew for a photo he bounded out from behind the desk where he was seated and placed his arm around me. A copy of the photo is below.

## Andy Pettitte Retires - No More "Core Four" (February 4, 2011)

Today marks the end of an era in Yankee baseball. Andy Pettitte, a member of the "core four" who led the Bronx Bombers to World Series titles from 1996 to 2009, is retiring from baseball at the age of 38. Pettitte retires with 240 regular season victories, as well as a major-league record 19 post-season wins. Aside from a stint with the Houston Astros, he spent the majority of his career with the number 46 emblazoned across his Yankee pinstripes.

His departure leaves the Yankees with a shaky rotation to begin the 2011 season, with a group of question marks following CC Sabathia and Phil Hughes. Quite frankly, after last year Andy would have been a big question mark even if had returned, but his experience would have served to assist the young pitchers. Last year he started with an 11-2 record, and was on pace to have the best statistical season of his career. A groin injury intervened, however, and he finished the season without seeing much action in the second half, not winning a game in the regular season after his return and then pitching, reportedly through great pain, in the playoffs. He won his last game as a Yankee against the Twins in the ALDS, and then pitched well but lost to Cliff Lee and the Texas Rangers in the AL Championship Series.

I was never the biggest Andy Pettitte fan. I never saw him as the staff ace, and believed (perhaps incorrectly) that he was not the big-game pitcher that the pundits made him out to be. True, he had the most post-season wins ever. But he also had the most post-season starts (42) and losses (10) in major league history as well. So there were times that he did not rise to the occasion. If I had been born twenty years later, there is no doubt that he would have been my favorite player; *a left-hander named Andy pitching for the Yankees?* That's a no-brainer. But I was not a kid when he began to pitch, and my view is that he was overly-hyped.

24

Now the discussion will begin, in New York, as to whether he should be elected to the Hall of Fame. The answer here is no. 240 wins is not sufficient. His career ERA of 3.88 is higher than any starting pitcher currently enshrined in the Hall, and his half-hearted admission to taking HGH several years ago will also work against him. His admitting that he took the drug, with his "aw-shucks" delivery, may have won over the fans who will continue to cheer for the "nice guys", but likely will not have the same effect on Hall of Fame voters who have, thus far, been loathe to admit anyone connected to the performance-enhancing drug scandals.

*****

Today the Yankees will hold a press conference where Pettitte will officially announce his retirement. The big question, undoubtedly, will be why he is retiring. There are three main reasons floating around the airwaves:

1) He does not believe that his body will enable him to pitch properly;

2) He wants to spend more time with his children;

3) He is concerned with having to testify in the Roger Clemens trial.

Early yesterday morning, Mike Francesa of WFAN stated that Pettitte was retiring because of lingering back and groin injuries. While his arm was in fine shape, according to Francesa, he was having such trouble with the rest of his body that he could not commit himself to pitching. Francesa stated that Pettitte's children wanted him to continue to pitch, but that he had decided to retire for medical reasons.

Later in the afternoon, however, ESPN's Michael Kay, a Yankees' announcer, stated on his show that Pettitte was retiring because of his children. Other whispers have focused on the upcoming Clemens perjury trial and the emotional toll that it will take on Pettitte. At today's press conference, I would expect that he will say that he wants to stay home with his children, and that his balky back did play a role – that if he cannot perform to the level that he expects of himself, he feels that it would be unfair to both himself and the team. He will not mention the Clemens thing unless specifically asked, and then try to brush off the topic as best as possible. That does not mean, however, that he is being 100% truthful.

The Clemens thing is interesting. The friends played together with the Yankees, went to the Astros together, and then reunited with the Yankees prior to Clemens' retirement. They apparently also took HGH and/or other PEDs together, and will soon meet again in a courtroom when Clemens faces charges of lying under oath. Pettitte has admitted to using HGH on at least four occasions. Clemens has completely denied using anything. The world believes Pettitte. The world does not believe Clemens. And ironically, it is his best friend's testimony that may finally nail Clemens. That is a great deal of pressure for Pettitte, perhaps even more pressure than he felt in his 42 post-season starts.

*****

Today's retirement officially breaks up the "core four" of Pettitte, Derek Jeter, Mariano Rivera, and Jorge Posada. It also serves to further the notion that the Yankees are an old team, and, based on their breakdown in last year's playoffs, little more than shadows of their former selves. Jeter suffered through the worst statistical season of his career in 2010, and Yankee GM Brian Cashman started a mini-firestorm by stating the obvious, that Jeter may be moved to the outfield in the future due to his decreased range at shortstop. Posada announced that he is bringing his catcher's mitt to Spring Training, even though the team has already informed him that he will be the full-time Designated Hitter this year.

Meanwhile, the Yankees continue to stockpile aging players. Perhaps in an attempt to revive their late 1990's magic (World Series titles in 1996, 1998, 1999 and 2000), they have signed three players who were all-stars in the late

1990's – pitchers Bartolo Colon and Freddy Garcia, and outfielder Andruw Jones. To expect any of these players to play a major role on a pennant-contending team would be folly. This is especially true for the pitchers. Garcia, for example, did win 12 games last year with the White Sox but he is little more than a five-inning pitcher. The Yanks already have one of those in AJ Burnett. Having two such hurlers in their starting rotation will prove overly taxing on the bullpen, even a bullpen which the team believes is stellar.

The other teams in the American League East have improved themselves this offseason. The Red Sox, who appear to be the class of the East, traded for slugger Adrian Gonzalez and signed speedster Carl Crawford. They can likely stake their claim to the division title once Spring Training breaks. The Rays, despite the loss of several key players and the bulk of their vaunted bullpen, did bring in Johnny Damon and Manny Ramirez to shore up their line-up and should contend for a wild card berth. And the Baltimore Orioles, riding the high of new (and former Yankee) manager Buck Showalter's leadership, went out and signed slugging first baseman Derreck Lee. They also traded for J.J. Hardy and Mark Reynolds, who will team with last year's core of Nick Markakis, Adam Jones, and Matt Wieters to create a formidable line-up. If any of their young pitchers perform to their potential, they can expect to finish in third place, ahead of the Yankees.

Today Pettitte retires as the second-best Louisiana native to pitch for the Yankees, behind Ron Guidry. He retires as the third-winningest pitcher in Pinstripes history, his 203 Yankee victories trailing only Whitey Ford and Red Ruffing. His teams won five World Series and eight League Championships. There is little doubt that his number 46 will soon join the other Yankee greats in the Stadium's Monument Park. They may retire the number quickly, or wait to do so with the numbers 2, 20, and 42 worn by his "core four" mates. Both Posada and Rivera should be retired by the end of the 2012 season, and Jeter, despite professing to want to play for another five years, will likely not make it that long.

27

More importantly for Yankee fans, however, is the likelihood is that these numbers will be retired before another Championship Banner is raised in the Bronx.

Today marks the end of an era in Yankee baseball, an era of success that may never be replicated in our lifetimes.

**Extra innings:  As for the "core four", Pettitte did return to the mound in 2012, only to suffer a fractured ankle and miss two months of the season. As the 2013 season begins, he is being counted upon, along with CC Sabathia and Hiroki Kuroda, to anchor the Yankees' pitching staff. Posada retired prior to the 2012 season, and Rivera missed most of 2012 after suffering what was initially thought to be a career-ending knee injury shagging flies in the outfield before a game. He is, however, returning to the mound for 2013, amidst rumors that he will be retiring after this season. Jeter had one of his best statistical seasons in 2012, and then suffered a broken ankle in the playoffs. He states that he will be ready to play by Opening Day 2013.**

# R.I.P. George Steinbrenner (July 13, 2010)

The morning has turned somber with the news that George Steinbrenner, principal owner of the Yankees, has died at the age of 80. Love him or hate him, all must agree that "The Boss" always had the best interests of the team in his heart. And while many blame him for the escalation of salaries in the major leagues, or for the disparity in talent between the "large-market" and "smaller -market" teams, George's legacy is far more than that.

No owner was more intimately involved in the running of the team; at times perhaps too much so. No owner took from his own pocket, when necessary, than the shipbuilder from Cleveland who purchased the Yankees almost 40 years ago. He will forever be villified by many, but will also be glorified by New Yorkers as the man who brought a winning team back to the Bronx.

They may have been "The Bronx Zoo" in the 70's and the workman-like team who captured a handful of titles at the turn of the century, but make no mistake, the Yankees have been, since 1972, George Steinbrenner's team. And all Yankees fans should be eternally grateful for his passion in building what he considered to be the greatest team in baseball history.

Rest in peace, George. Hopefully you will be watching tonight's All-Star game with the rest of the storied Yankees: Babe, Lou, Mickey, Joe D, and your old friend Billy.

**Extra innings:** If I had taken the time, I could have penned a much longer and thorough obituary for King George. I preferred, however, to do a simple, short, and immediate post.

## Gary Carter Succumbs to Cancer: The "Kid's" Ironic Death (February 17, 2012)

Baseball great and Hall of Famer Gary Carter, affectionately known as "the Kid", died of brain cancer yesterday at the age of 57. Carter started his career with the Montreal Expos, but gained perhaps his greatest fame as a key member and co-captain of the 1986 World Champion New York Mets. In what may be one of sports' greatest ironies, the religious ex-catcher, who fought his disease with such class and bravery, is now dead while the plethora of drug-abusing teammates who shared his Shea Stadium dugout are still around to mourn his loss.

Dwight Gooden. Darryl Strawberry. Lenny Dykstra. Keith Hernandez. A veritable drug "hall of fame", these were the men, along with Carter, who led the Mets to their first championship since the franchise's magical 1969 title. It is also the last time that the Mets have captured baseball's ultimate prize.

In 1985, "The Kid" joined the Mets, slugging a tenth-inning, opening day home run off of St. Louis' Neil Allen (ironically, a reputed alcoholic who had been traded by the Mets for former MVP and alleged cocaine-user Hernandez). Carter's flair for the dramatic had already been cemented in 1981, when he slugged two home runs in the All-Star game - the first game played after the player's strike which split the baseball season into two sections. Another two-home run game highlighted Carter's performance in the 1986 World Series, and he retired in 1992 after a 19-year career which featured 2,092 hits, 324 home runs, and 1,225 RBI's to go with his .991 fielding percentage. He also singled to begin the famous rally in the 1986 World Series, which culminated with Mookie Wilson's ground ball going through Bill Buckner's legs and led to Game 7 and the Mets' championship. Without Carter's two-out single, there would have been no rally, no chance for Buckner's error, and the Red Sox would have won the Series in six games.

An eleven-time All-Star, Carter's all-around excellence is perhaps best borne out by the fact that he was selected for the "Silver Slugger" award, as the National League's best hitting catcher, on five occasions between 1981 and 1986. He was also awarded the "Golden Glove", for fielding excellence, three times. He currently ranks sixth on the all-time list for homers by a catcher. Carter was elected to baseball's Hall of Fame in 2003, becoming the first player to don an Expos' hat on his plaque in Cooperstown. His number 8 jersey was retired by the Expos in 2003.

Left behind to mourn Carter, in addition to his family, friends, and fans, are former teammates Gooden, Strawberry, Dykstra, and Hernandez. Together, this was the nucleus of a team that, by all rights, should have completely dominated baseball from the mid-1980's through at least the mid-1990's. Instead, it is a team which captured only one title, and is a prime example of wasted potential.

The "poster children" for this waste are Gooden and Strawberry, both of whom electrified both the City of New York and the entire baseball world with the early promise of their careers and both of whom fell well short of their expectations, instead succumbing to the temptation of drug excess. Both captured the "Rookie of the Year" awards with the Mets, and both later achieved a later World Series ring with the Yankees, of all teams. Gooden actually pitched a no-hitter while with the Yankees, and Strawberry eventually amassed 335 homers in his career. But both also had well-documented bouts with drug abuse, both have seen the inside of jail cells, and both simply failed to fulfill their potential. Of that, there is no question. Either one of them could have been the best ever at their position. Neither came close.

Dykstra, with his "popeye-like" physique and bouts of rage, was the quintessential steroid user of the 1980's. He achieved great success with both the Mets and Phillies (he was second in the league's MVP balloting in 1993), but it is now evident that such success was due to anabolic, rather than work-ethic, reasons. He later achieved further fame as an investment advisor, but, like his baseball success, this was built on fabrication and his investment business crumbled. He later pled guilty to bankruptcy fraud, and was sentenced to house arrest.

The last of the drug-four, Hernandez, was the co-winner of the 1979 Most Valuable Player Award. He won a World Series championship while a member of the Cardinals in 1982, won the batting title in 1979, and was named to two All-Star teams while a member of the Redbirds. Widely acknowledged as the best fielding first baseman of his era, he began a string of eleven consecutive Gold Glove wins in 1978. Why, then, was he traded to the Mets before the 1983 season for the above-mentioned Allen, who, at best, was a middle-of-the-road pitcher? One word – cocaine. Allegations of cocaine use dogged Hernandez, so much so that the Cardinals were forced to trade their Gold Glove-winning first baseman during the off-season following their 1982 championship run. Hernandez served as co-captain of the 1986 Mets with Carter, and has enjoyed a second career as baseball broadcaster.

Note that it is not my intention to suggest that any of the other four players deserved to die instead of Carter, nor is this intended to be an indictment of the 1986 Mets and their failure to win more than one title. I simply find it ironic that we are today mourning the loss of Carter, while the others, who polluted their bodies so openly and for so long, taking gambles with their health on a daily basis, are still here.

Then again, New York's own Billy Joel sang that *"Only the Good Die Young"* - it is perhaps fitting, therefore, that the man known as "the Kid" was taken so young.

Extra innings: Since Carter's death, the only one of the four other players referenced above who has continued to make adverse headlines is Lenny Dykstra. In March 2012, two weeks after Carter died, Dykstra was sentenced to a three-year prison term after pleading no contest to three counts of grand theft auto. Then, in July of 2012, he pleaded guilty in federal court to three separate felonies – bankruptcy fraud, concealment of assets, and money laundering. These were based on his efforts at hiding and/or selling over $400,000 worth of assets that he did not reveal in a bankruptcy filing from 2010. On December 3, 2012, he was sentenced to six and a half years in prison, 500 hours of community service, and was ordered to pay $200,000 in restitution for these crimes.

# SECOND INNING

## STEROIDS AND OTHER DRUGS

Few stories have had such staying power as the continued allegations of Performance Enhancing Drug usage by ballplayers. Some of the game's biggest stars have been named as having been linked to PED-supplying companies, and players have continued to receive suspensions for violating the league's anti-drug policy despite the many warnings given to all about the use of such substances.

One of the posts concerns Ryan Braun, who was profiled in the prior chapter. Braun allegedly tested positive and was able to avoid suspension due to what some consider a technicality. A person subject to far greater scrutiny is Alex Rodriguez, who has an entire chapter in this book devoted to him; in 2009, he admitted to the use of such PED's in the early 2000's, before he arrived in the Bronx. Recently, however, his name has surfaced in connection with a large drug supplier based in his home town of Miami; as of this time he has scrupulously avoided speaking to the media, and rumors are rampant that he may have played his last game in pinstripes.

This year's Hall of Fame voting, which resulted in no players gaining election and which is the subject of the last entry in this chapter, seems to show a hard-line approach being taken by the baseball writers as to suspected drug users, whether the allegations against them have been proven or not. Even players who simply played in what is called "the Steroid Era" were barred from induction this year, setting up what will no doubt be a very interesting election process in 2014.

# Hey Big Papi - Como Se Dice "Accountability"? (August 10, 2009)

Another star baseball player is alleged to have tested positive for performance-enhancing drugs. Another star baseball player states that he will properly address the allegations. Another star baseball player fails to stand up and be properly accountable for his actions. As Yogi Berra said, "It's déjà vu all over again".

This time, the player in question is David Ortiz of the Red Sox, a/k/a "Big Papi". He is the hulking, teddy-bear-like Dominican who, with his gaudy home run and RBI numbers, has been the biggest and strongest hitter in Red Sox nation for several years now. He is also a player who has, in the past, condemned those players who had relied on steroids in order to boost their playing level. But we shouldn't throw stones, Papi …

Recently it was revealed that the big guy, along with his former teammate, uber-malcontent Manny Ramirez, are on the mystery list of ballplayers who tested positive for some form of performance-enhancing drug in 2003. It was the same secret list that contained Alex Rodriguez's name, as well as about 100 others. The fact that Manny was on the list caught nobody by surprise, especially since he had already earned a nice 50-game vacation this year for taking drugs either intended to enhance his performance or lose that extra pregnancy weight. It appears that either is a violation of baseball's drug policy, so there was never a need to clarify why he was taking it in the first place.

But Papi? Surely the Sox' leader, an outspoken critic of juicers, could not have been injecting himself or taking anything improper. When the story was leaked he promised that he would come clean, and tell the truth about whether or not he had actually taken steroids. And the world waited with baited breath for this beacon of veracity to speak his mind. His explanation …

First, we need to flash back several months. Earlier this year, the Yankees' (and arguably baseball's) best hitter, Rodriguez, was linked to the 2003 list. Approximately one week later, he gave a supposedly-candid press conference where he blamed his cousin for giving and injecting him with an unknown substance. He didn't know what it was, he said. He didn't know that it was improper, he said. He didn't even know that he had tested positive in 2003 until now, he said.

And Alex Rodriguez is no hulking teddy bear. To the contrary, he is tabloid fodder, as his imperfections have played out splendidly in the world's biggest media outlet and his every misstep has been chronicled for the ages. So when he issued what amounted to little more than self-denial, everyone smirked. Not only for the implausibility of the story itself, but that it took a week to concoct that story. A week, no doubt, of speaking to his lawyer, his agent, the players' union, and every other person who could have scripted a better tale for him to weave. And in the end, nobody believed him. But because everyone understood the drug culture that infested baseball at that time, they moved on. Yes, they call him "A-Roid" on the road. He is playing, though, the Yankees are winning, and the continued distraction from the allegations has been minimal.

Surely, one would think, David Ortiz would do better than Alex Rodriguez. He would just come out and tell the truth, tell the children what (if anything) he had done and move on from there. Just having his name linked to the report is a taint on his career, as I have noted in a prior piece. He could only come out on top in one way – by telling the truth. New England loves him. The truth would likely free him from further scrutiny. Surely, one would think that David Ortiz's handlers would advise him to tell the truth.

One week later, after no doubt meeting with his attorney, agent, and the player's union representatives, Papi held a press conference in, of all places,

New York, to make the following announcement: "I definitely was a little bit careless back in those days when I was buying supplements and vitamins over the counter - legal supplements, legal vitamins over the counter - but I never buy steroids or use steroids."

And some people apparently believe him. But why? How did his "account" differ in any way from A-Rod's? Break it down. He didn't know what it was, he said. He didn't know that it was improper, he said. He didn't even know that he had tested positive in 2003 until now, he said. Sound familiar? Of course it does. The only difference is that Ortiz is beloved in Beantown and throughout baseball (except in New York) and Rodriguez is reviled for his selfish play and the fact that he plays for the "Best Team that Money Can Buy."

Despite the fact that he has his believers, there simply is no accountability in Big Papi's world. Here, when faced with the chance to really address the issue head-on, he pulled the same hide-your-head-in-the-sand act famously employed in the past by Mark McGwire, Rafael Palmeiro, countryman Sammy Sosa, Roger Clemens and Rodriguez. How refreshing it would have been had he simply fessed up to taking something in the past. The man went from platoon player on a bad Twins team to the star of the Sox. A friend of mine has been yelling for years that Ortiz had to have been using steroids. His career would not have been derailed by the truth.

To the contrary, his candor could have unshackled the silence which has marked baseball's tacit acceptance of such drug usage. It could have led to the eventual release of the bad-boy list so that all names would be revealed, at which point others could have taken similar paths of truth, which could, possibly, have led to the end of the witch hunt that has marked the past couple of years of the "steroid era". Instead, his empty proffer provided us with the same garbage answer that has been fed to the public since the steroid story broke some years ago, again certifying how baseball, in general, has still yet to properly condemn the cheaters.

But the fact that he refuses to be held accountable for his own actions should not truly shock nor surprise anyone. That is the current American culture. Nobody wants to be held accountable for his or her own actions. In a world where you must navigate through voice mail systems and dozens of voice mails before speaking to a live person at many large companies, the idea of "accountability" is a dying one. In a country where the government has been forced to spend billions of taxpayer dollars to bail out companies and entire industries, and where the top executives continue to reap financial windfalls, the idea of "accountability" is a dying one, much like the idea of a public person being candid about his improper activities before they are revealed by others. So perhaps asking him to take responsibility is simply too much.

We have all heard the stories. The woman who spilled Dunkin' Donuts coffee on her lap and sued, the high school girl from Florida who blamed others for the picture of her going commando in her high school yearbook, the hundreds of thousands of children who will say, at least once today, "It wasn't me".

Perhaps if Papi had given his "excuse" before being linked to the report, then it would have seemed more believable. If we are to take him at face value, then he apparently knew he was taking supplements and vitamins, at least some of which were bought in the Dominican (also similar to Rodriguez's story, by the way). Why he never owned up to taking these in the past, and only did so in response to an allegedly positive test, must force us to question his veracity. It is not a question of New York v. Boston, or of the "Evil Empire" v. "Red Sox Nation".

It is simply a question of morals. David Ortiz, like so many before him, chose not to tell the truth. He, like the others, is hiding behind a smokescreen of carefully-chosen words. The difference is, he said that he would tell the truth. And many believed that he would, even as it took him about a week to formulate his version of the truth. As such, his failure to properly address the allegations before him is even more offensive.

Then again, the man is hitting .219. This could be the most "offense" he generates this year.

Como se dice "it's my fault", Papi Chulo? For some reason, I doubt that you know the answer.

**Extra innings:** Ortiz's 2009 season was not a total disaster, despite my comments above, as he finished with a respectable 28 Home Runs and 99 RBI's. Those numbers increased to 32 and 102, respectively, in 2010. He slugged 29 homers to go with his 96 RBI's in 2011, and posted his highest batting average in years, .309. An injury-plagued 2012 season, however, ended with him amassing only 23 homers and 60 RBI's. During the off-season, he signed a new multi-million dollar contract to remain with Boston, presumably to end his career as a (smiling) member of the Red Sox.

# Why is Mark McGwire Discussing the Past? (January 12,2010)

It has now been almost 24 hours since the not-so-startling announcement by Mark McGwire that he used steroids throughout the 1990's. I have spent several of those hours in the car, listening to the local sports radio stations in order to hear the pundits' takes on the various issues concerning his statements. And while most of them have gotten bogged down in the obvious, precious few minutes have been spent discussing the most critical aspect of this announcement.

Note from the outset that I will not use the words "news" or "confession" in this writing. First, that Mr. McGwire used steroids is anything but news. He merely confirmed what everyone suspected, or "knew", already. And he really did not give a true confession. He admitted using steroids, but stated that he did so solely to heal from injuries. Inexplicably, in the midst of his alleged mea culpa he adhered to the belief that he did not gain any competitive advantage through his use of injections or pills. Those items, he told Bob Costas last night, do not help hand-eye coordination or, in and of themselves, hit a baseball. Maybe that is true, but they gave him those popeye arms that helped launch hundreds of baseballs over fences in major league parks throughout the time that he was juicing.

Some points that bear mentioning, however:

1) Why now? Almost a decade after his retirement from baseball, and five years after he infamously refused to "discuss the past" before Congress, why did Mark McGwire, in January 2010, decide to alert the media to his past medicinal steroid usage? Conventional wisdom posits that he did so in anticipation of becoming the St. Louis hitting coach this year; and that by addressing the issue now (if you could call it that) he would avoid a media circus in Spring Training and thereafter. More likely, however, it seems to be what will turn out to be a futile attempt at gaining induction into the Hall of

Fame; the timing of this announcement a scant week after the most recent election results were published cannot go unnoticed. No doubt he saw his voting percentage continue to languish in the 20% level and decided it was time to do something about it.

2) Word on the street is that Cardinal Manager Tony LaRussa, who has acted like nothing short of a surrogate father for the fallen slugger, intends to activate the big lug in September and October and use him as a pinch-hitter. A clever man, that LaRussa, because even one at-bat will make the 'roiding Redbird an active player again. As such, it will be another five-year wait before he can even be considered for the Hall of Fame, and then he gets fifteen more bites at the election apple, hopeful that by then the next generation of baseball writers will better understand his pain and contrition.

3) Nobody seems to have consumed more of the kool-aid in this instance than LaRussa. His staunch defense of McGwire, his favorite player, including his denials of McGwire's steroid use have, until yesterday, seemed to completely defy logic. Now, he believes that through this single "admission" everyone else will join him and the love-fest that was engendered in 1998 will be reborn. His exact words were that Mark will hopefully regain his "stature". Apparently he has not noticed that those arms and shoulders have shrunk to mere human size since they have been steroid-free, so the large "stature" will never be regained. Also, when asked why he would hire McGwire as a hitting coach, he pointed to how McGwire became a better hitter as he aged. I guess he continues to deny that this "progress" was artificially induced.

4) Dave Kingman on steroids. That's who Mark McGwire was. And since "King Kong" has never merited any serious Hall of Fame consideration, then the same should be true for "Big Mac". He was nothing more than an average player who hit a lot of home runs. And if you take away the steroids and increased power, then it is certainly feasible that many of those prodigious blasts

would have been little more than flyouts, which would have pushed his career batting average even closer to the Mendoza line, the majors' bright-line test for hitting futility (.200). Even a tearful almost-I did a bad thing speech can't change that.

5) If the owners had a Hall of Fame, that would be a completely different story. The injection-fueled 1998 home run race between McGwire and his steroid sidekick, Sammy Sosa, put tens of thousands of fannies into the seats during the summer of 1998 and saved Major League Baseball from an almost-certain oblivion in the wake of earlier work stoppages. The lords of baseball lined their pockets with millions of dollars which can be directly attributable to the actions of these two men and their pharmacists. To those owners, therefore, Mark McGwire and his syringes would be first-ballot Hall of Famers.

6) Which leads to the ultimate, and, arguably, most important, point. This is not a steroid issue. Many players took steroids during the time that is now wistfully referred to as baseball's "steroid era", and many more will fess up in the future. Nor is it a Hall of Fame issue, because, quite candidly, his statistics, even with his home run totals, do not measure up with those faces already hanging in Cooperstown's halls. Rather, the issue is that of the athletes/celebrities and their patent refusal to be held accountable for their own actions.

In this case, aside from saying that he did not use steroids for an improper purpose, it is clear that Mark McGwire, five years after failing to tell the "truth" before Congress and almost a decade removed from the game over which he cast a large shadow and, later, a black cloud, seems to believe that he is now to be completely absolved of any wrongdoing.

Apparently he called Roger Maris' widow (remember, be broke Maris' single-season home run record) and told her that he was sorry, as if that would change anything. While the Maris family has taken the classy and high road in the wake of the events of the last 24 hours, the reality is that poor Mark is anything but sorry. He knew what he was doing. He knew what substances he was placing into his body, even if he claims now that he doesn't recall specifics. He also knew that his arms and upper body were growing into Hulk-like proportions, and that this growth spurt was directly attributable to his use of steroids.

His scripted statement, as well as the rehearsed statements thereafter, did little more than parrot the sincere confessions of players before him, like Andy Pettitte and Alex Rodriguez, who admitted using performance enhancing drugs and provided reasons such as injury and rehabilitation in support of their rationales for such use. It's all too convenient for Mark McGwire, who once reigned as baseball's single-season home run king, to do the same. There is so much more that he could have said. But his handlers and the St. Louis Cardinals' brass probably told him not to say more.

So yet again we have a star athlete who seems to believe that a single "oops" comment will erase everything that he has done in the past. That the lords of baseball will once again shine their spotlights on him as he returns to the Cardinal bench as a glowing reminder of baseball's past, and that an additional 50% of the sportswriters who cast annual votes for those enshrined in Cooperstown will, for the first time, look favorably on his application so that he may walk into those hallowed halls as a member, and not simply as an ostracized cheater. That by waiting until the time was right for his own purposes, he could still salvage what little dignity he apparently thought he still had and proudly wear the red-and-white uniform again. As Pete Townsend sang in "Tommy" – "see me, feel me, touch me, heal me".

But that is all too convenient. His statements of the last 24 hours should do nothing to change the perception of Mark McGwire that has resonated through baseball for the past five years, that of a coward, of a man who cheated and who consistently refused, even before the United States Congress, to come clean. For his statements are not those of a man who intends to "come clean", but are rather those befitting a person who is being forced to admit to something that he still believes was not wrong. His comments that steroids did not affect his performance are beyond laughable. And he should be vilified not only for making those statements, but for thinking that the public is stupid enough to actually believe that he was attempting to repent for those sins.

Better yet, let's all take a page from his playbook. Let's refuse to talk about the past. Let his record be limited to his performance on the diamond in 2010 and beyond. If he turns out to be the best hitting coach or manager of all time, then open the Hall's doors for him on that basis. And if he does get to pinch-hit this year, and gets a hit in his only at-bat, then he can retire with a career batting average of 1.000. Then he'll have something to brag to his children about.

**Extra innings: McGwire served as hitting coach for the Cardinals for several years, but was never activated to hit in a ballgame. He is now the hitting coach for the Los Angeles Dodgers. The baseball writers have still refused to elect Mark McGwire to the Hall of Fame, and his poor showing year after year in the balloting leaves no indication whatsoever that he will ever gain enshrinement. In the last election, he garnered less than 17% of the vote. He is perilously close to being removed from the ballot.**

# HGH Testing and the Delicate Arms of Major Leaguers (July 23, 2010)

Through the miracles of modern science, there is a blood test that can now detect Human Growth Hormone (HGH). The real question appears to be whether or not there is a HGH testing procedure that won't harm the delicate arms of major league baseball players.

HGH testing has been instituted in the minor leagues, as announced by MLB Commissioner Bud Selig. This puts baseball at the forefront of drug testing, as it is the first major US sport to conduct such tests. According to the Commish, blood will be drawn from the non-dominant arms of players who are not currently on a major league club's 40 man roster. Then the samples will be whisked off to Salt Lake City, where they will be tested for the presence of HGH.

No such testing has been introduced at the major league level, and will not be started until agreed upon between MLB and the Players' Union. And while the public does not appear to be insisting on such tests, it would seem like a good idea for the players' union to embrace the idea of such testing, to further clean up their image to the fans.

But to truly embrace something, the players will need two good arms. And that is where at least one player is finding difficulty with the testing idea. Yankees player representative and centerfielder Curtis Granderson said that any proposed testing procedure would have to be fine-tuned before the union would agree to such testing. And while he mentioned factors such as how often the test would be given and to whom, his real concern lies elsewhere.

You see, Curtis is worried about getting a bruise on his dainty and delicate arm. While he should be more concerned with getting splinters in his posterior from sitting on the bench so long due to his lack of production and playing time, Mr. G. frets that, if the blood is not drawn perfectly, he may have a little discoloration on his inner elbow. And that could adversely affect his post-game shower or ability to properly hit the post-game buffet, I guess.

According to Curtis: "We have (blood testing) during our spring training physicals where depending on who is administering the needle, sometimes they get it right and you move on and it's not problem... Sometimes they get it wrong and you bruise up and swell up a little. Those are some of the things we want to be careful about and make sure it's as accurate as possible."

Seriously. He is worried about bruising up and a little swelling – after the game! I would assume, but do not know for sure, that there must be an ice cube or ice pack somewhere in the vicinity of major league locker rooms that such bruise/swelling sufferers could easily avail themselves of. And I assume that these ice cubes/packs are given to the players for free, so it is not like they even have to pay for them.

The perception of the spoiled ballplayer can only be strengthened by such stupid comments. Yes, it is true that if a player has a truly serious reaction to a needle it could impact their playing. But what are the odds of that happening? To Curtis and his fellow Yankees? Come on! No doubt the Yankee brass can fly in the best phlebotomists in the nation to draw the blood from his fragile veins. And they can hire the most experienced nurses to gently, carefully place a band-aid over the little spot of blood that may trickle out afterward. Maybe they can even use a special band-aid, with medication on the underside of it, to prevent any potential bruising.

Man up, Curtis, and stop whining. Focus on hitting the ball, and not on such petty stuff. It only makes you look like a prima donna. A prima donna who is paid millions to play a kid's game, and often not very well. I would do that for the money, and let them take blood from me before, during, and after the games.

Shut up and make a fist.

46

Extra innings: Granderson was singing a different tune in November 2012, in the wake of a year which saw him slug over 40 home runs and raised suspicions about whether he was using steroids or other performance enhancing drugs. In a phone interview with the New York *Daily News*, Granderson said that: *"when people do something that seems abnormal, the first thing people say is, 'He must be on steroids' … I got it this year, that the reason I was able to hit home runs this year is that I must be doing something."*

He then added, with respect to HGH testing that had been agreed to in baseball's latest Collective Bargaining Agreement, *"I don't think too many people are as familiar with HGH, but they consider it a steroid. To let people know we're testing for that and anything else that can be a performance-enhancer, we're trying our best to keep it out of the game and we're going to have strict penalties for anybody caught using it."*

He also expressed amazement that allegations about baseball players and performance-enhancing drugs were so rampant, as opposed to football, where the players are larger: *"You never hear it talked about in football, where most guys are massively bigger than us, or in basketball… It's amazing of the three major sports, we're the ones that are consistently talked about when it comes to that stuff, so hopefully we can get rid of that conversation. The fact that everyone is going to get tested in spring training is going to be the beginning of getting things going and wiping everything clean from the sport."*

During a pre-season game on February 24, 2013, Granderson was struck on the right arm by a pitch, and sustained a fractured right forearm which doctors said would keep him out of the lineup for at least ten weeks. They did not disclose, however, whether the forearm had been previously weakened by the drawing of blood or by any other HGH-related tests.

## Braun's Positive Drug Tests a Negative for Jews and Baseball (December 14, 2011)

Three weeks ago *(see Chapter One)*, I wrote a piece heralding the beginning of a new era in Jewish baseball history, a charge being led by three all-star players, Kevin Youkilis, Ian Kinsler, and the eventual winner of the 2011 National League MVP award, Ryan Braun. Three weeks ago, Jews across this country could look to that threesome, especially Braun, the Brewers' slugger, with pride. Three weeks ago, Jews were able to celebrate their first baseball MVP award in almost a half-century.

But that was three weeks ago. This past weekend, the "golden era" of Jewish baseball, as it was termed by this writer, suffered a major setback with the news that Braun faces a 50-game suspension at the beginning of the 2012 season. According to reports, Braun violated baseball's substance abuse policy, and as such is subject to the automatic suspension. It has been reported that Braun failed two separate tests, each of which showed elevated levels of testosterone, and both of which also showed a synthetic component to the elevated levels.

Initially, I wanted to give Braun the benefit of the doubt, that this was a false positive. He labeled the positive tests as "B.S.", and a statement was released by his management team, which stated that there was no "intentional" violation of baseball's anti-drug policy. Braun has been a stellar player for five years now, racking up gaudy statistics while never being held under suspicion of ingesting any illegal substances. There has been no startling change in his physique, like the popeye-like arms that were brandished by Mark McGwire and Jose Canseco or the swollen head of Barry Bonds. Also, baseball has presumably cleaned up its act, strengthening its drug testing programs and procedures, so it seemed impossible that he could have been using steroids, right?

It is possible that the tests were incorrect, or that Braun had taken some other substance, innocently, which led to the positive results. In reality, however, for me to suspect that he was truly innocent is little more than reverse discrimination. In the past, any players accused of drug usage have been immediately vilified by this writer and others, my own beliefs surrounding the guilt of these players completely bypassing the presumption of innocence that I preach for my clients. So for me to do so here, based solely on his (and my) religion, would make me the ultimate hypocrite, and I will therefore not protest Ryan Braun's innocence.

Assuming that the drug tests are valid, and that Braun does face this suspension, the positive tests will have a broad range of adverse ramifications: baseball as a whole will be tarnished, especially with the news that he knew of the positive tests before he was even named as MVP. The presumed aura of a "cleaner" baseball society will be exposed to be fraudulent. The Brewers' franchise and its offensive firepower, already facing the loss of slugger Prince Fielder, will be further decimated by the loss of Braun for what will amount to be almost a full one-third of the 2012 season. Obviously, Braun and his own personal legacy will be forever harmed, even if the tests are proven to be wrong, because the mere suspicion of drug use, as we have all learned, is a tough hurdle to overcome.

Lastly, the positive tests will have a potentially adverse effect on the Jewish people. First, it will create a sense of disillusionment in the people who looked up to Braun as a model for our people, a people who have struggled mightily to have athletes to hold up as role models for our children. Those superstars have been few and far between. The 1930's-1940's were dominated by Hank Greenberg. He passed the *yad* (a small, baton-like implement shaped like a hand with an outstretched finger used to mark a person's place while reading the Torah) to Al Rosen, who in turn begat Sandy Koufax in the 1960's. The early 1970's brought us swimmer Mark Spitz, who rose from the horrors of the 1972 Munich Olympics as a true Jewish hero, capturing seven gold medals even as Palestinian terrorists murdered eleven members of Israel's Olympic squad. The late '70s featured Rod Carew, who apparently never really converted to Judaism but whom we embraced as our own regardless, and Shawn Green hoisted the religion on his shoulders thereafter.

Until the current crop of all-stars, there was a void. Adam Sandler did his best to fill that void with his trio of Chanukah songs, aimed at listing the Jews in Hollywood and elsewhere to, as he sang, provide little Jewish children with a sense that they were not alone during the Chanukah, and Christmas holidays. Those songs, however, contained very few athletes. He included the afore-mentioned Carew and Olympic skater Sarah Hughes; the other two athletes named, however, were O.J. Simpson, whom he was quick to label "not a Jew", and former Oakland Raider QB Daryle Lamonica, who was included simply because his name rhymed with the holiday.

*****

Sandler's recitation of actors, singers, and other entertainers, however, did not provide a great deal of surprises. Jews have always had a presence in Hollywood, both in movies and television, and there have been a plethora of Jewish singers. From the Marx Brothers and Three Stooges to Rodney Dangerfield and Joan Rivers to Jerry Seinfeld, Jewish comedians have made audiences laugh for decades. Nobody has ever questioned the Jews' abilities to make people laugh, especially with their own brand of self-deprecating humor. And with respect to Hollywood, nobody has ever questioned the Jews' ability to be overly dramatic.

*****

So why is it so devastating that Braun may have cheated? There is an ever-present fear among the Jews that anti-Semitism, which still exists throughout the world, will be heightened in the wake of any scandal involving a Jewish person. Many people breathed a collective sigh of relief when the Jewish people were not blamed for the Bill Clinton-Monica Lewinsky scandal. Thankfully, the mention of her religion was not a featured part of the stories about her, as some had feared. The same is true for the Bernie Madoff scandal, which could have been used by some to fuel the stereotypes of alleged Jewish greed. And now, if Braun is exposed as a cheater, it can provide more fodder for anti-Semites to point to how Jews are unable to succeed at sports without cheating; this, clearly, would be a vicious and incorrect statement, but is not beyond the realm of possibility.

Is it wrong for Jews to try to look to their own for heroes, whether on athletic fields or otherwise? For many Jews, it is no different than people looking to athletes from their home countries. So many Jews fled from and remain disenfranchised from their home countries that their religion has become their "home" identity, so for a Jewish boy to look to Ryan Braun as his hero is no different from the Italian child who reveres last year's MVP, Joey Votto.

Then again, the true religious zealot would argue that it *is* wrong. The first of the Ten Commandments states that *"Thou shalt have no other Gods before Me"*. Could it be, then, that God provides us with a superstar athlete once a decade or so, a man of such awesome ability that he rises above those around him (Greenberg, Koufax, Spitz, Braun) simply to test us? Is it possible that worshipping these athletes as heroes is therefore a sin, and that God has sent a message to us through Braun's failed drug tests that people are not to worship athletes?

A truly religious Jew would likely make that argument. So would former NBA superstar (and non-Jew) Charles Barkley, who famously stated that "I am not a role model." Perhaps God simply chose Barkley to deliver his message several years ago, and when that was not properly heeded, he was forced to take matters into his own hands through a more blatant means.

Perhaps.

Extra innings: Braun was eventually cleared of the allegations, based on a flaw in the "chain of command", or handling, of his samples. To some, this is merely a technicality. Braun's performance in 2012, however, showed that he was capable of amassing stellar numbers without the use of PEDs, as he led the National League in Home Runs, Slugging Percentage, and Runs Scored while again winning the Silver Slugger award and reaching the 30-30 club (30 Home Runs and Stolen Bases) for the second consecutive season. He finished second in the MVP voting in 2012, behind San Francisco's Buster Posey. Prior to the 2013 season, he was named in a list of players linked to a PED facility in Florida, but denies the usage of any such PED's, stating that he consulted with the facility only for assistance in refuting the prior positive test.

## Melky, Bartolo, Testosterone and the Rocket Man Returns (August 23, 2012)

Over the past two weeks, two high-profile major-league baseball players, San Francisco outfielder Melky Cabrera and Oakland pitcher Bartolo Colon, have been suspended by Major League Baseball due to drug tests which showed elevated levels of testosterone. No doubt the Bay Area has been rocked by these suspensions, especially since it was the home base of BALCO, the company at the center of baseball's biggest drug/steroid scandal of several years ago, the scandal which ruined the reputations of baseball players and other athletes including home-run king Barry Bonds, Gary Sheffield, Benito Santiago, and Olympic sprinter Marion Jones.

Cabrera and Colon, however, share much more in common than their current Bay Area locations. Both are from the Dominican Republic, where several players have undergone "questionable" treatment methods in the past, and both, perhaps not remarkably, have seen their statistics markedly improve over the past couple of years. Cabrera, for example, went from a 2010 season in which he totaled only four home runs and a .255 batting average to a stellar 2011 campaign in which he blasted 18 homers, had 87 RBI's, stole 20 bases and batted .305, a fifty point jump over the prior season. This year, with the Giants, he was hitting .346, tops in the National League, already has knocked in 60 runs, and was the All-Star game MVP, leading the National League to victory and ensuring them of home-field advantage in this year's World Series.

The 39-year-old Colon, whose best days were from 1998 through 2002, totaled only 14 victories between 2006 and 2009, and then sat out 2010 before being picked up off the scrap heap by the Yankees in 2011. The seemingly rejuvenated Colon barely made the team coming out of Spring Training, but ended up starting 26 games and finishing with eight victories, a season which led to a contract with Oakland and a 2012 season in which he has already tallied ten victories.

The other common thread? Both recently played for the Yankees. Cabrera's career in the Bronx ended after the 2009 season, and Colon did not begin playing for the Bronx Bombers until 2011. Still, it is a link that cannot be ignored. While the hope is that the testosterone suppliers did not emanate from the Bronx, the possibility still looms large. Whether or not the genesis of their drug usage can be traced back to their days with the Yankees may be revealed through further investigation, and if additional players test positive a definitive link may be drawn. Remember, many of the players listed in the Mitchell (steroids) report played at one time or another for one of the New York teams.

Hopefully history will not repeat itself and the suspensions of these two players will be an aberration rather than the start of a whole new round of drug-related suspensions and allegations. Time will tell.

*****

Steroid quiz time – It was announced that former major-league (and Yankee, sense a pattern here?) fireballer Roger "Rocket" Clemons will be pitching for a minor-league team, with hopes of pitching later this year for his hometown Houston Astros. The reason for this "comeback" is:

a) Returning to the major leagues, armed with cups of clean urine, will be the ultimate "f#$% you" to federal prosecutors who wasted millions of dollars of taxpayer money in their futile attempt at convicting Roger on perjury charges;

b) Roger wants to be known forever not as a steroid abuser, but as the only man to start and win a major-league game at the age of 50; even if he is pitching in meaningless late September games for the team with the worst record in all of baseball;

c) Roger really is simply a ruthless competitor who wants to prove to himself and the fans that he is capable of still pitching in the majors;

d) Roger wants to delay his appearance on the Hall of Fame ballot;

e) All of the above.

The answer, of course (for our purposes), is (e). He wants to clear his name; his competitive nature is unquestioned; but, most importantly, pitching in a game for the Astros will delay his eligibility for the Hall of Fame. Clemons last pitched in the majors in 2007. As such, he will be on the next Hall of Fame ballot – a player is eligible for election five years after their last appearance. So why wouldn't Clemons want to be on the ballot?

Steroids. True, he was never officially convicted of using performance enhancing drugs, at least not in a court of law. In the court of public opinion, however, this "rocket" was using some illegal or improper forms of fuel and, if the past couple of years are any indication, this perception will keep him from having a plaque hung in the Hall of Fame.

People with gaudy, drug-enhanced statistics such as Rafael Palmeiro and Mark McGwire are already sitting on the side, their noses pressed to the front doors of the Cooperstown shrine with little or no prospects of ever gaining entry. And, as of now, there are a trio of alleged steroid users (Clemons, Barry Bonds, and Sammy Sosa, all of whom testified before Congress along with the finger-wagging Palmeiro and memory-deficient McGwire), who all retired after the 2007 season and are all facing certain denial at the next election.

If Clemons does appear in a game for Houston, even if only to pitch to one batter, that would toll his eligibility for another five years, until at least 2017. By then, he likely believes, the furor over the steroid era will have abated or sufficiently waned to allow the baseball writers to elect him for entry into the Hall.

As is always the case, time will tell. Should the recent suspensions of Cabrera and Colon lead to a rash of penalties for other players for elevated levels of testosterone or other performance enhancing drugs over the next several years, however, the perception of major league baseball as a drug-riddled sport will not go away. If that happens, Clemons' exclusion from what he no doubt believes to be his rightful place in the Hall of Fame will result, regardless of when he is first eligible for election.

**Extra innings:** Clemens did not pitch in the majors last year, and did appear on the Hall of Fame ballot – but, as noted in the next post, did not garner enough votes for election. In an interview from February 18, 2013, Clemens said that he did not care about whether or not he was elected to the Hall, stating that: "I'm not going to lose any sleep over it. If those guys [the baseball writers/electors] feel I deserve to be there, then I deserve to be there. If they feel I don't, then that's okay, too."

This appears, however, to be little more than lip service or the work of a spin doctor ventriloquist, pulling the strings to the Rocket's mouth. Clemens was, according to various reports over the term of his career and afterward, greatly concerned with his reputation; for him to now say that he does not care whether or not he is elected to the Hall of Fame seems completely at odds with his past fanaticism concerning his image and accolades.

As for the Yankee link that I noted between Colon and Cabrera, it appeared to be more than simple coincidence when both were named in documents seized from a Miami-based PED supplier. Also named in the documents were Yankee players Alex Rodriguez and Francisco Cervelli; all have denied any wrongdoing.

Cabrera, meanwhile, defied the maxim that "crime doesn't pay" by inking a two-year, $16 million contract to play with Toronto during the off-season. The same can also be said for Colon, who somehow earned a raise when he re-signed with Oakland for the 2013 season.

The sad reality is that when cheaters like Cabrera and Colon profit from their actions, as was the case with their new contracts, it only serves to validate the belief, based on a pure risk-reward analysis, that it is worth it for players to gamble being caught taking performance enhancing drugs. When players believe that they can take these PED's in order to give them an "edge" over the others, or merely to keep pace with the others fighting them for a roster position, it is, to a certain degree, difficult to question their actions.

Testing or no testing, it appears that major league baseball players are, for the most part, quite adept at staying one step ahead of the testing mechanisms. Such was the case with HGH, where so few were caught and punished even though it is fair to assume that it was being used by many, and no doubt there is, today, another steroid-like booster out there that is being used by players and for which tests are not being administered.

## Baseball Hall of Fame & Lance Armstrong - Needles Everywhere (January 12, 2013)

It has been quite a week for the endlessly-intertwined worlds of professional sports and performance-enhancing drugs. Days ago, the Baseball Hall of Fame voters emphatically slammed the doors to their hallowed building in the faces of players who used such drugs, were accused of using such drugs, or who merely played in an era where such drugs were prevalent. In so doing, the now holier-than-thou baseball writers shunned baseball's all-time home run king, the man widely considered to be one of the greatest pitchers of all-time, and, in a true case of collateral damage, a man who amassed more than 3,000 hits while maintaining a squeaky-clean image.

That Barry Bonds and Roger Clemens were denied entry into the Hall was no surprise. After all, the voters have sent clear indications over the past several years that the "cheaters", for want of a better term, would not be granted the privilege of having their visages embossed on Hall of Fame plaques, at least not for now. But for people like Craig Biggio, the newfound "rules of entry" proved to be quite damaging. Biggio now stands as the only eligible member of the heretofore elite "3,000 hit club" who is not enshrined in Cooperstown. This is so despite the fact that Biggio has never been accused of using any form of performance-enhancing drugs. It is a clear case of "guilt by association," and is an indictment on the voters that he was denied entry.

Biggio did garner the most votes of any candidate, but fell 39 votes short of election. The next highest vote-getter, former pitcher Jack Morris, finished three votes behind Biggio. For Morris, one of the greatest pitchers of his time and the man behind possibly the second-best game ever pitched in World Series history (an epic 1-0, Game 7 victory for Minnesota over Atlanta in which he hurled 10 shutout innings, capturing the title for the Twins and earning him MVP honors) election on this ballot had a sense of urgency – next year will be his fifteenth, and last, time on the ballot for election. He also has been swept up, it appears, in the tidal wave of anti-drug sentiment, even though he has never been accused of engaging in such improper conduct.

## A. Good Guys v. Bad Guys

I previously wrote of a "double standard" of sorts for performance-enhancing drug users. Those who were friendly and amiable, I argued, were more easily forgiven by the public and the world of baseball. Due to this "double standard" well-liked players like Andy Pettitte, who actually admitted to using HGH, and David Ortiz, who was accused of using PED's, could smile their way through their admissions or denials and not lose any of their stature with the baseball public. On the other hand, players were who not well-liked, especially those disliked by the press, would be vilified at every turn. Such was the case with malcontents like Manny Ramirez and Alex Rodriguez.

The Hall of Fame vote, seemingly, proved my point. Witness the votes garnered by seven accused steroid or other PED users:

| Player | # of votes | % of vote |
|---|---|---|
| Jeff Bagwell | 339 | 59.60% |
| Mike Piazza | 329 | 57.80% |
| Roger Clemens | 214 | 37.60% |
| Barry Bonds | 206 | 36.20% |
| Mark McGwire | 96 | 16.90% |
| Sammy Sosa | 71 | 12.50% |
| Rafael Palmeiro | 50 | 8.80% |

Note the disparity in the voting totals. One could argue that the accusations involving the top two, Bagwell and Piazza, were not as loud as the others and that they were not involved in the congressional hearings regarding steroid use. I would also argue, however, that they were the nicest and friendliest of the bunch. The truth is that rumors about their usage were fairly wide-spread for some time; both went from normal-sized to gigantic in a short period of time, *a la* Bonds, and certainly much more than simple weight-lifting would have permitted. But they were nice. That's the key.

In contrast, both Clemens and Bonds were surly, combative, and often disliked by the press. They are viewed as the poster children for the steroid era, and, despite being widely considered among the best at their profession, face a large uphill battle for induction. But they still amassed significantly more votes than the bottom three men above, partially because their statistics and accomplishments were greater but also, no doubt, because of external factors.

McGwire, who famously refused to discuss "the past" before Congress, later recanted his denials and admitted to the use of improper substances. To some, it was a catharsis. To others, it was too late. Yet Big Mac still sits in a major league dugout, having left St. Louis to be the Dodgers' hitting coach. It appears, however, that he is allowed to wear a uniform but will never gain proper entry into the Hall. Sosa was a smiling bear cub for years, but his testimony before Congress was comical at best (he pulled out the *"No hablo ingles"* card in order to avoid properly testifying) and the backlash continues.

Worse, still, was Palmeiro. Defiantly wagging his index finger at his inquisitors, he emphatically denied the use of any form of performance-enhancing drugs. Sometime later, however, while with Baltimore, he tested positive for such drugs. In what seems to be little more than a case of "you made us look really stupid", the baseball writers have saved their greatest wrath for poor Rafael. Only 8.8% of the vote is an abysmal showing. This is especially true for someone who is one of only a handful of players to have amassed 500 home runs and 3,000 hits in a career. Even if we delete his last two seasons in Baltimore, when we *know* that he was using such drugs, he still garnered 2,800 hits and 520 home runs; certainly Hall of Fame statistics, and better than players like Bagwell and Piazza, who, as noted above, placed much higher than him in the voting.

So, it seems clear that the writers are not only barring those who allegedly used drugs (famously, none of them have been actually "convicted"), but are also establishing a pecking order of the accused based on their personal feelings toward same. At the same time, however, they appear to be harming players who seemingly played clean, like Biggio and Morris, while clogging the Hall of Fame ballot for years to come. According to Buster Olney of ESPN, this will prove even more of a problem next year – all of the players on this year's ballot will be back (except for Dale Murphy) and they will be joined by several people who should be Hall shoo-ins, like former teammates Greg Maddux and Tom Glavine, neither of whom were ever linked to such substances. One could argue, in fact, that Maddux should be the first unanimous election of all-time, having amassed staggering statistics without the aid of PEDs, while pitching to batters who, by some counts, were all (or almost all) using some form of synthetic assistance. The following year will bring still more candidates, including Randy Johnson, whose statistics rivaled Maddux's and could also be considered a possible unanimous selection.

**B.  A possible solution**

I profess that I am torn on whether the "accused" should be allowed into the Hall, or whether, they should be allowed with a special "steroid-era" designation on their plaques. Mere accusations cannot form the basis for denial, but the evidence against players like Clemens and Bonds, despite their apparent Teflon-status in the courts, screams guilt. On the other hand, there are players like Piazza and Bagwell who were victimized, it seems, by the whispers against them even though those allegations did not rise to the levels of those such as Bonds, Clemens, Sosa, and McGwire. And even if players did use, what if they amassed Hall-of-Fame caliber statistics before being caught, like Palmeiro?

The Hall of Fame Committee must make a definitive decision on these players. To allow them on the ballot, clogging the process and at the whim of the voters, seems to be a non-response to the issue. Realistically, if 26% or more of the voters (remember, a player needs 75% of the votes for induction) are truly hell-bent on never electing a player even *accused* of steroid use, then those players should simply be removed from the ballot. Let the voters decide who should be removed from the ballot, thereby removing the logjam and permitting the election of others. It would be a one-time decision as to each player, as opposed to the 15 years of denial that can result if they are left on the ballot.

And if those who are removed from consideration seek some form of retribution, such as filing court action to be reinstated to the ballot (how ludicrous a waste of the court's time would that be?) then let a court determine if these players can or cannot be considered for election to baseball's most esteemed building.

To continue to leave their fates in the hands of vindictive voters, the same writers who, by all counts turned a blind eye to such drug usage only a decade or so ago, seems equally ridiculous.

## C. Lance Armstrong – "Please love me again"

Now, today we have the news that disgraced cyclist Lance Armstrong plans to admit that he engaged in blood doping during his record run of Tour de France titles. In what is clearly little more than an attempt at salvaging what may be left of his career and reputation, Armstrong, who has fiercely denied rumors of impropriety for years in spite of a mountain of evidence to the contrary, is apparently willing to confess to the world, via an interview with Oprah Winfrey, that all of his protestations have been lies.

Armstrong hopes, obviously, that people hear his contrition and think back to the smiling face of US Postal Service cycling, the cancer survivor, and the person who formed the "Livestrong" Foundation and raised millions of dollars for cancer research. And if they do, he reasons, then, like Messrs. Pettitte and Ortiz, he may be forgiven. He must hope, however, that the general public does not recall the person who, in his vehement denials, threw teammate after teammate under the proverbial bus, his false cries of innocence leaving a wide swath of damaged reputations and careers across the competitive cycling spectrum.

Armstrong may find himself, unwittingly, in the same position as baseball's all-time hits leader, Pete Rose. For years, the player known as "Charlie Hustle" denied the rumors of his having bet on baseball games, even after he accepted a lifetime ban from baseball. He did so, like Armstrong, in the face of evidence which not only suggested, but clearly showed, his guilt. Finally, after years of denials, Rose admitted, in a book, to the gambling. To the world of baseball, however, it was too late to come clean, and Rose is still banned from baseball, the gates to the Hall of Fame still slammed shut.

More importantly, Rose's confession was too late for the court of public opinion. That should cause Armstrong some worry, because it is that court that he will be pandering to with his no doubt crocodile-tear laden confession, which will be, according to reports, broadcast this Thursday. He will not be reinstated to competitive cycling, nor will his seven Tour de France titles be returned to him after his mea culpa. He is doing this all for the fans, for the public, and for his reputation. Like Pete Rose before him, however, the better likelihood is that his pleas will fall on deaf ears.

**Extra innings:  At least one former baseball player hailed the "no-vote" – former reliever and Hall of Famer Rich Gossage called for the exclusion of any accused PED users from the Hall of Fame. According to reports, Gossage said that:** *"I'm glad nobody who is tied to performance-enhancing drugs got elected … It's cheating. You've got two players, one using, one not.*

*You have two different animals."* He also took direct aim at Barry Bonds and his single-season and career records for home runs: *"The most sacred records in baseball were Hank Aaron's 755 homers and Roger Maris' 61-homer season. I think they ought to reinstate those records. They stripped Lance Armstrong of his seven Tour de France titles."*

Lastly, Gossage said that if a known steroid user were to gain election, *"I may never go back to Cooperstown – it wouldn't be a sacred hall anymore."*

As for Armstrong, his interview with Oprah was anything but a success in the court of public opinion. According to many radio personalities and written reports, he came off as cold and calculating – characteristics that did not, and likely will not, engender any public sympathy or forgiveness.

# THIRD INNING

## ALEX RODRIGUEZ – "A-ROD"
## OR LIGHTNING ROD?

Over the past two decades, no Major League baseball player has been the subject of greater scrutiny, or has been more polarizing, than Alex Rodriguez. This has been especially true for the three-time Most Valuable Award winner during his nine-year tenure with the New York Yankees. His alleged drug usage has been discussed in the prior chapter, and his history of post-season difficulties is examined in the next chapter. A 14-time All-Star and ten-time winner of the Silver Slugger award, he has played the unwitting villain to Yankee Captain and media darling Derek Jeter since he first donned the Yankee pinstripes, and his continued missteps have only served to fuel the tabloid fires. Interestingly, these two posts deal with the rehabilitation of his image - but he has since returned to the proverbial doghouse.

The recent allegations of PED usage, which come at a time when he is already expected to miss half of the 2013 season, if not more, while recovering from off-season hip surgery, could spell the end of his Yankee career and his stint as main albatross to the team's ownership.

## A-Rod and K-Hud -- Enough Already!! (October 8, 2009)

**Pre-Game Notes:** The 2009 baseball playoffs were telecast on TBS. The producers spent an inordinate amount of time showing Kate Hudson in the stands. At the time, the actress (and daughter of actress Goldie Hawn) was dating Alex Rodriguez, the Yankees' superstar third baseman. I penned this fictional letter in response to the camera time being given to Ms. Hudson.


An open letter to the lords of TBS –

*We know. We've known for a while. Alex Rodriguez has an actress girlfriend. But here's the thing – we don't need to see her during the ballgame.*

*Because, Mr. Producer, as you may be aware, Alex Rodriguez (affectionately known as A-Rod) has long been a lightning rod for media and tabloid fodder, especially since his arrival in New York several years ago. His well-publicized rifts with teammates, his all too public philandering, eventual separation from his wife, and this past season's steroid allegations have placed him squarely on the back pages of the New York tabloids on an almost daily basis through the beginning of this season.*

*But then something happened. When he returned to the Yankees this spring after a hiatus to rehab his hip (and image), he was a different A-Rod. From the mammoth home run that he blasted in his first at-bat of the 2009 season, it was apparent to the Yankee faithful that this was no longer the brooding loner who focused only on his own personal statistics. All of a sudden, number 13 was a team player, committed to helping the others around him win, and an active participant in dugout celebrations.*

*This metamorphosis did not go unnoticed, and his teammates seemingly rallied around him. His once-cool relationship with Derek Jeter, the Yankee Captain, seemed to thaw, and one by one the players openly lauded his efforts and contributions to the team. No longer was he the king of the solo home run when the team was already ahead by six runs. Now, his hits mattered. It was noted during a game last week, for example, that he had the most go-ahead or tying home runs in the major leagues this year.*

*So even though he was seen about town with his new starlet girlfriend, the latest in his string of blondes (Toronto stewardess, Madonna, etc.), the media covered their new romance only for a while. And soon, thankfully, that quieted down in favor of his efforts on the field.*

*And now it is October. It is the time for heroes to step up and lead their teams to the promised land. In the Bronx, it is the month that evokes names like Reggie Jackson and Derek Jeter, those who have stepped up their games to bring the coveted World Series trophy home to New York. October has never been synonymous with success for Alex Rodriguez. Quite to the contrary, his performance in the past few playoffs has been anything but successful. Going into last night's game, he had been hitless in 20 at-bats with runners in scoring position. Not quite the production that was expected of him, and he has served as scapegoat for the team's failure to win the World Series since his arrival.*

*Last night, he broke out of that slump in a big way, delivering two key hits in the victory over the Twins. The first was delivered at a critical time, and gave emphatic notice that the new A-Rod was here to play, even though the calendar says that it is October. And as he rounded first base, Mr. TV Producer, how nice would it have been if we had been provided with a shot of his reaction to his ripping that monkey off of his back? No doubt he at least cracked a bit of a self-satisfied smile. Or how nice would it have been if we had been provided with a shot of the Yankee dugout, to see how his teammates reacted to his timely* and productive hit? No doubt it would have made for good television to see how this team has now embraced the man that they formerly scorned.

Yes, it would have been nice, but instead, we were "treated", and I use the term loosely, to a shot of the girlfriend in the stands. There was Kate Hudson (let's call her K-Hud) clapping away at her man-of-the-month's big hit. And while it wasn't as egregious as all the years of Fox's self-promotion during their televised games (shot after shot of the new season's TV show stars, for those who remember) there was simply no reason to go down the path of A-Rod's personal life at this time. The newspaper articles leading up the playoffs have focused on the new Alex. Kate's presence has barely even been mentioned in articles over the past few weeks – because nobody cares anymore.

And then they showed the clip again, twice, leading into commercials. It was quite the little montage. The Jeter homer. The A-Rod hit. The K-Hud clap.

I guess that there are those who do not know of the budding romance – "Hey Mabel, look there. Isn't that the girl from Laugh-In? Wow, does she look young for someone her age". But let's face it, denizens of TBS, the people who are watching the game do not care that Kate Hudson is there, nor do they need to see her every game. And I don't recall seeing camera shots of the other wives or girlfriends, or even Mr. Jeter's parents in their familiar Yankee Stadium box.

Plus, this has not exactly been the longest romance of all time. It is rumored that she is pregnant (little A-Rod?) but, in reality, her dating an athlete was little more than an inevitability. She was married to a rock star. Her dalliances with actors are legendary, and one breakup allegedly caused poor Owen Wilson to attempt suicide. Athletes were the last group of celebrities that she hadn't sampled. Let's see if they have legs. When they are married for a few years, show her. Then again, after a few years it won't be newsworthy anymore, I guess, so it won't do anything to boost your ratings.

68

*If I want to watch Kate Hudson, I will rent "Almost Famous", or worse, force myself to sit through "You, Me and Dupree" again. I won't turn on a baseball game.*

*In sum, Mr. TBS (and to the producers of the stations that will show the later rounds), I would hope that the Yankees advance and Alex continues to garner timely hits and contribute to Yankee victories. But – please don't feel the need to show Ms. Hudson every time he does so. We already know.*

*Sincerely,*

*Someone who is watching the game for the game's sake*

**Extra innings:** Not surprisingly, the romance did not last. K-Hud is now engaged to a musician, Matthew Bellamy, and the two have a son together. A-Rod is reportedly dating ex-professional wrestler Torrie Wilson, although he has kept a very low profile recently while rehabilitating from hip surgery so, at least for the past couple of months, they have not been seen out in public together.

## <u>The Continued Exorcism of Alex Rodriguez</u> (October 18, 2009)

It was, quite literally, a watershed moment. In the middle of a driving rain, Alex Rodriguez and his Yankee teammates continued to exorcise their worst demons with a hard-fought, late-night, epic battle with their arch-nemesis, the ironically-named Angels. And while we cannot overstate the importance of two baseball games, the reality is that they played out as if scripted by the best of Hollywood writers, even if it is the favored team that is defying all odds by winning.

From the first week of April, Yankee fans fear an inevitable October showdown with the Halos. For reasons that remain unknown, the business-like approach that the Yankees take to the game always seems to self-destruct in the face of Mike Scioscia's team, as the Angels and their players act as kryptonite to the Yankees' perceived aura of invincibility. At least twice in the last several years, a seemingly better Yankee squad failed to advance to the next round of the postseason, its season stopped at the hands of John Lackey, Chone Figgins, and company.

So when the Yankees captured the first game Friday night, it was not yet cause for celebration. In each of the prior two series between these teams, history told us, the Yankees had won the first game only to then self-destruct and lose the series. But something was different Friday night, there is no doubt to that.

Perhaps it was the cold, but temperature is still no excuse for the mental mistakes committed by the Angels, such as the pop fly that landed in front of Erick Aybar that led to the second (and, eventually winning) run. As it may have read in the Angels' almost-hometown paper of *Variety*, "California Club Coughs Up its Cool in the Cold of the Cathedral". It was, in short, a game decided by three Anaheim errors, a very un-Angelic game in the field. And sometimes

70

that's what it takes when two titans clash – that victory is decided when one blinks, or simply commits an error.

But any euphoria from Friday night would have completely evaporated in the wee hours of this morning had the Angels captured game two. It would have meant the loss of the all-important home field advantage and a long plane ride to the West Coast, one in which the Yankees would have faced the inevitability of yet another playoff loss to the Angels and another long off-season of perceived failure.

Instead, the purest of all Hollywood moments played out before our bleary, sleep-deprived eyes. You could almost visualize a movie director perched in his chair high above, barking out orders: "Alright people, this is it. This is the shot that's gonna make us millions. Picture this - the home team is down by one. We're in the grand palace of baseball, the giant structure known to many as the Cathedral, and, in a twist of fate or religion, the Angels are in town. It's the big, salary-laden Yankees against the cute, monkey-mascot Angels. And the Yankees are down to their last three outs.

"Let's make it even more interesting, and send up the biggest hitter they have – and let's make it a guy who, before this year, never even got a hit in the playoffs, if you read the newspapers and listen to the commentators. He's got the weight of the world on his shoulders, and if he fails, so does the entire team. And just for added effect, let's give him a Hollywood girlfriend. Everyone wants to see this guy fail, right?

"But let's make it even better – cue the rain. Not a drizzle, but a hard-driving, cold rain that chills everyone in the stadium to the bone. I want to see breath, people! I want drama! Let's make magic!"

And - roll tape - the scene begins. The much-maligned A-Rod steps to the plate and blasts a homer just beyond the outfielder's reach, and trots around the bases to the waiting arms of his teammates in the dugout while the cold, drenched crowd whips itself into a frenzy.

The Yankees eventually won the game in the 13th inning, taking seemingly commanding two-game lead in the series. But time will forget the winning run. We will forget that Jerry Hairston Jr. (who?) scored on yet another misplay by an Angels' infielder on a sharply hit ground ball by Melky Cabrera.

Time will not forget the tying home run. Highlight reels for years to come will remind us of that blast. For that was the true watershed moment. It was the moment when Alex Rodriguez, again, shook that monkey (rally, 800 pound gorilla or otherwise) off of his back and pushed his teammates closer to the promised land. This has been his playoffs. His demons are exorcised, even if the Yankees do not win another game in 2009.

Fox Sports showed its flair for the dramatic by replaying the home run, again and again, in slow-motion. Watching the swing of the bat and the ball rocketing over the outfield fence, with A-Rod surrounded by slow-moving raindrops as big as the stitches on the ball, was the stuff of which Hollywood magic is made. It was reminiscent of Roy Hobbs' epic home run in "The Natural". And we couldn't have scripted it better.

**Extra innings: Apparently exorcised demons can return. Rodriguez is now undergoing rehabilitation following hip surgery. He is doing so in New York, as team management is doing its best to keep him as far away from his teammates as possible. Rumors swirl as to whether he will ever play in another game for the Yankees following his latest link to possible PED usage.**

# FOURTH INNING

## POST-SEASON VICTORIES AND LOSSES

It is said that admission is the first step to recovery. In this case, it is critical for us to admit that Yankees' fans are baseball's most spoiled and jaded fans. Anything less than a World Series title leaves the Yankee faithful dissatisfied. Even when the team does win the championship, as it did in 2009, the fans' barrage of criticism continues up until the final out is recorded. Witness the posts from 2009, when the Yankees beat the Philadelphia Phillies to win the last of their 27 World Championships.

Many fans, this writer included, place the blame for the past three years of post-season failures on the shoulders of the team's manager, Joe Girardi. Like his predecessor, Joe Torre, Mr. Girardi seems, too often, to rely on his notebooks full of statistics rather than trying to consider the human elements of the game. My contempt for many of the decisions made by the man I refer to as "Joe-Bot" is evident throughout this chapter. It continues through today.

These posts essentially run into one another, so, for most, there is no need for commentary thereafter.

## **<u>Yankees Pull Even - While the Fans Snooze</u> (October 30, 2009)**

Like the people in the Yankees' bullpen not named Mariano Rivera, I spent the eighth and ninth innings of last night's game drifting in and out of consciousness. Not that the game was boring, mind you, but it was simply too late. These are the times when it would be easier to live on the West Coast – waking up at 6 to go to work and staying up until almost midnight watching a game is difficult once, but on consecutive nights is it downright cruel.

I was able to haul my achy body out of bed this morning, however, and, after having downed my coffee, am coherent enough to provide some observations on last night's game.

1) The first two games have proven that good pitching will beat good hitting. This World Series features two teams that combined for over 460 home runs during the regular season, by far the most in World Series history. And yes, four homers have been hit so far, but all have been solo shots and, with the exception of the Yankee bullpen implosion in Game 1, these solo homers have accounted for almost all of the teams' offense. All four starting pitchers have turned in excellent performances, a string which may come to an end Saturday night when the teams move to Philadelphia and the bandbox known as Citizen's Park.

2) Luckily for the Yankees, Joe Girardi seems to have misplaced his notebook of pitching match-ups. Rather than witnessing the usual trot-out of the lefty-righty-lefty relievers that he usually feels the need to parade before the Stadium faithful, he went to the bullpen only once, so that Mariano Rivera could obtain a rare two-inning save. Of course, this begs the question of how often this can be done, and, moreover, is there anyone else in the bullpen that he even trusts? Or whose psyche and arm he hasn't already destroyed?

3) His counterpart, Phillies' manager Charlie Manuel, clearly seemed to have misplaced his notebook on Pedro Martinez. It does not matter how well Pedro was pitching in the sixth inning. Any Yankee fan knows, and his own manager should know, that Pedro hits a concrete wall at his 100th pitch. He may have thrown more pitches in a game this year on occasion, but back when he was a card-carrying, Don Zimmer-tossing member of Red Sox Nation, he would self-destruct immediately following his 100th pitch. And last night, right around his 101st pitch, he gave up a hit to the mightiest of the Yankee hitters (cough cough), Jerry Hairston, Jr. Let's face it, even Nick Swisher could have gotten a hit at that point. But that hit, and Manuel's error in leaving a tiring Pedro to pitch, led to the run that put the game out of reach.

4) A similar lapse of judgment was shown by Yankee outfielder Johnny Damon, a former teammate of Pedro's in Boston. Swinging at the first pitch when Martinez was clearly tiring was a rookie mistake, not what one would expect from a seasoned veteran, and directly counter to the patience that he is supposed to exhibit at the plate. And a feeble pop-out to end an inning? Not quite the outcome that he was hoping for. Perhaps if he had looked at a couple of pitches, to get Pedro closer to the century pitch mark, the Yankees could have put the game away in the sixth.

Now the series shifts to the City of Brotherly Love, where the Yankee pitchers will have to take their licks at the plate (remember, they only use the Designated Hitter in the American League ballpark) and Hideki Matsui, the Yankees' usual Designated Hitter, will ride the pine of the bench waiting for his turn to pinch hit. At least Yankee starting pitchers Andy Pettitte and CC Sabathia had prior stints in the National League (Pettitte with the Astros and Sabathia with the Brewers) so they have a concept of how to hit, and Sabathia has even shown some power in the past. The more interesting question will be for game 5 – if the Yankees go with Sabathia in Game 4, as expected, will we see beleaguered AJ Burnett in Game 5, or the much-ballyhooed World Series debut of Chad Gaudin? And if Burnett pitches, will Jose Molina, his personal catcher, be allowed to hit (well, more appropriately, go to the plate and make an out) or will Girardi feel the need to keep Jorge Posada's bat in the line-up? Time will tell.

As for me, it's time to catch up on some sleep tonight. Obviously I am going to be up late Saturday and Sunday watching the games. And Sunday, the television will be set to Fox for the entire day. With the big Giants-Eagles game at 1:00 and the Bret Favre coming-home party at 4:15, coupled with Game 4 at 8:00 or so, my wife is going to have to peel me off of the couch around midnight.

Good thing my first court appearance Monday is at 11 – making it on time for a 9:00 would be questionable. Then again, Joe Girardi could always pull me out and substitute a righty for me if he liked the match-up.

# Yanks Go Up 3-1; But Don't Pop Those Corks Yet (November 2, 2009)

The Yankees, as everyone no doubt knows, have now jumped to a 3-1 lead in the World Series over the Phillies. But it is still too early for Yankee fans to open their Champagne bottles and hoist Joe Girardi's number 27 jersey to the rafters. For this is not the "commanding lead" that some pundits would have you believe, especially if the winds of momentum again begin to blow in a Southwesterly direction to the land of Cheesesteaks and Rocky Balboa. There is still, potentially, much baseball yet to be played.

Some perspectives on the weekend's action:

1. Alex Rodriguez appears to have found his groove again, as he engages in his own personal game of "hit or be hit". His final tally for the weekend series – three HBP, two HR, and one ninth-inning, tie-breaking double. And his restraint in not rushing at Phillies' hurler Joe Blanton after being hit last night was also admirable. He has truly (finally) evolved into a team player, and may capture the MVP trophy that he deserved, but which eluded him, in the AL Championship Series.

2. The Phillies, meanwhile, appear to be playing as if they are a basketball team – they seem to be operating under the belief that a "big three" can somehow raise them to victory without any assistance whatsoever from their teammates. Without insulting any of the other 22 men who donned the red pinstripes this weekend, the only Philadelphians earning their salary in this Series are Cliff Lee, Chase Utley, and Jayson Werth. Others have had hits here and there, but outside of those three, their impact has been minimal. And unlike basketball, usually a team requires more than three contributors – especially when only one of the three is a pitcher who can legitimately pitch once only three or four games.

3. In fact, if you remove Utley from the Phillies' lineup, Yankees' starter CC Sabathia has only surrendered one run in his two starts. Utley has hit three homers off of him, and also slammed a monster double in the first inning (which may have been a homer in the Bronx) which led to the first run last night. To use a past line from the Phillies' one-man quote machine, Pedro Martinez, Utley has been Sabathia's daddy in this Series (*recall that Martinez referred to the Yankees as "his daddy" following a defeat when he was still with the Red Sox*). No doubt Chase is chomping at the bit for a Sabathia re-match in Game 7.

4. This was another weekend without sleep. Even with daylight savings time, we did not get a respite from the late-night games. The lords of baseball, in their obvious conspiracy to rob the PA-NY corridor of any rest, rained down torrents of water over Citizen's Bank Ballpark Saturday, forcing an eighty-minute rain delay before Game 3 even began. So, we still were in the hole for twenty minutes when it came to the all-important sleep. Don't the baseball denizens know that we need our six hours a night?

5. I have a partial solution. Let's forget about playing Game 5. Cliff Lee is pitching for the Phillies, and if ever there was a *fait accompli*, this is it. There is simply no way that the Yankees can beat him in Philadelphia, so let's just forget about playing the game and place it in the win column for Lee. Look at it this way - the enigmatic AJ Burnett is pitching for the Yankees. He already had his good game for the Series, to the surprise of many, so it is more than a distinct possibility that he will self-destruct tonight. And assuming that Jose Molina is catching for him, despite Jorge Posada's valiant attempt at keeping his starting role with the final two-run hit last night, the Yankees will only have seven hitters to face the already dominant Lee (discounting Molina and Burnett, of course). And that is if you even bother counting Robinson Cano, who, when last seen, was looking at his bat like it was some type of foreign object.

78

And to sweeten the idea for Phillies' fans, we can even make up statistics and help some guys out – we can make it a 4-2 victory for Lee. He pitches his eight innings, strikes out 10, and gives up two runs, one unearned. Brad Lidge gets a save, so he gains some confidence back, and we can even say that first baseman Ryan Howard finally broke out of his slump, did not strike out at all, and even hit a two-run homer. It seems fair, and it will let us get some sleep tonight.

6. I am beginning to feel sorry for Chad Gaudin. The mocking of Gaudin is starting to get downright cruel. The current plan is for Andy Pettitte to pitch Game 6 for the Yankees. Today on the radio, they asked one of the "experts" about this decision. He replied that it might be a problem because Andy is older and has had a tired arm in the past, but that "well, it's either him or Chad Gaudin".

Next, you will hear someone say something like "If Andy can't go, you might see the Yankees try to coax eighty-something year-old Whitey Ford out of retirement to pitch Game 6. I mean, he is really old, hasn't pitched in over forty years, and can barely lift his arm above his head. But, he has World Series experience, holds the record for most World Series victories, and, well, it's either him or Chad Gaudin". Apparently being the number four starter on this Yankee squad is no great badge of honor. Poor Chad.

7. In reality, Game 6 of the Series, assuming Lee works his magic tonight, will be the most important game, or at least the most important game since Game 3. Because in a Pedro Martinez-Andy Pettitte matchup, which means a game featuring late-30's starters who cannot survive more than six or seven-innings, the bullpens might be called on to decide the game. And neither manager trusts his bullpen occupants right now, except for Girardi's unrequited love for Mariano Rivera. So the likelihood is that one team will have to jump out

to an early and insurmountable lead if it is to win Game 6 without having to bite off their fingernails with fear over the last three innings.

And if the Phillies ride Pedro's no-more-than-99-pitch coattails to victory over Mr. Pettitte, the momentum shift will clearly be on the side of the reigning World Champions. Then, even if CC Sabathia trots his large frame to the mound to face arch-nemesis Utley and his slumbering teammates Thursday night, anything can happen. Sometimes even the better team falters in the face of enough momentum and pressure. And if it gets to Game 7, the pressure will be squarely on the broad shoulders of CC, A-Rod, and the other Bronx Bombers. How they will react, if it gets that far, remains to be seen.

**Extra innings:** **Luckily for the Yankees, they captured Game 6 and won the series, four games to two. Since then, however, they have failed to taste World Series success and remain "stuck" at 27 championships; which is not enough for a fan base clamoring for title number 28.**

**Unfortunately for Alex Rodriguez and his fragile psyche, he was not voted as the World Series MVP – losing out to teammate Hideki Matsui. Then again, Matsui was not brought back to the Bronx for the 2010 season, despite his heroics, so perhaps Rodriguez had the last laugh. For a while, at least, as other posts in this book would seem to indicate.**

## American League Playoff Preview - the Race to Philadelphia (October 6, 2010)

*Fast forward to the 2010 playoffs. The Yankees were the defending champs, but, as always, their fan base, had grave doubts about their ability to repeat. This post was a preview of the 2010 American League playoffs.*

Tonight, four American League teams begin their battles to determine who will be offered up as sacrificial lambs to the juggernaut that is the Philly Phillies. Each team will carry a 25-man roster, but, realistically, the hopes of each squad rest squarely on the shoulders of one or two of its members. It is best to highlight those players, and how their teammates, to the extent that they are able, may make the difference between a winning or losing effort.

**SERIES ONE – TWINS v. YANKEES**

Minnesota Twins: The Twins have the unenviable burden of drawing the team that has completely dominated them over the past several years, unceremoniously sending them home last October. Mired in a nine-game post-season losing streak, they also shape up as the one team that the Yankees can beat in a short series, which might explain the Yankees' seemingly voluntary fall into the Wild Card position.

Their key player is Joe Mauer, who is, quite simply, the best offensive catcher in the game today and who may retire as the best ever. Clearly, as he goes, so do the Twins. With fellow All-Star Justin Morneau still out due to lingering effects from a concussion, Mauer is the driving force (with occasional help from the ageless Jim Thome) behind Minnesota's offense.

From the mound, the player to watch is Carl Pavano, known to his opposition as the $40 million mistake. The man who had more injuries than victories during his four-year Bronx tenure may have the pleasure of beating his old teammates in Game 2 at home, and will avoid the wrath of the Yankee

Stadium crowd. He could prove to be the difference in a five-game series, and nothing would make the late George Steinbrenner turn over in his grave more than a victorious Pavano.

New York Yankees: The defending champions limped to the finish line, perhaps intentionally, to avoid a first-round matchup with the Rangers. Despite boasting the best offensive lineup in the AL, their thin starting pitching may prove to be just the tonic for a Minnesota club yearning for post-season success.

You can completely disregard any discussion about the Yankees' offensive might. Whether or not the Bronx Bombers live to see the ALCS will depend on the arms of four people: CC Sabathia, Andy Pettitte, Phil Hughes, and Mariano Rivera. For them to move on, Sabathia will have to win at least two games in each series. Period. No questions asked. He must win every time he takes the mound. Without his two victories, the Yankees can start booking their vacations and golf tee times as early as next week.

But even with CC winning two games, either Pettitte or Hughes will also have to emerge victorious. The question with each is whether they have the strength to do so. There is no question of Pettitte's mental toughness. His aging body, however, combined with the possibility of a cold Minnesota evening (or two if the series goes five games), may spell disaster for the postseason's all-time winningest pitcher. And Hughes? He has already exceeded his pitch limit for this year; and his efforts during the season's second half barely resembled the horse who tore through the league before the All-Star break.

And then there is Mariano, the greatest closer that major league baseball has ever seen. For the last couple of weeks, though, he has looked uncharacteristically human. He will need to elevate his game to Rivera-like levels again or face blowing a game that the Yankees can ill-afford to lose.

**Prediction: Yankees in Four**

## SERIES TWO – RAYS v. RANGERS

<u>Tampa Bay Rays</u>: Baseball's new "it team" also crawled across the finish line last weekend, finishing first in their division almost despite their best efforts at losing the crown. Their pitching staff is likely the best of the four remaining AL squads, but their once-formidable hitting has two big question marks heading into playoff action.

Evan Longoria is the key for this team, but he has been sidelined with a quad injury since September 23rd. If he is not 100%, or close to it, by tonight he has little chance of success against Rangers' ace Cliff Lee. And that means two games with no production from their star third baseman, which could prove to be the death knell for the Floridians.

Rumor has it that the Tampa police have begun an all-out search for Carlos Pena's hitting prowess. Local milk cartons have pictures of his bat as being "missing", while the few dozen Rays' faithful ponder how their slugging first baseman could muddle through September with a batting average hovering around .170. Pena has to realize that guys like outfielders Carl Crawford (playing for a contract) and B.J. Upton could help carry the team during the floundering stretch run of its regular season, but he will have to step up and find his groove now for the Rays to continue to the next round.

<u>Texas Rangers</u>: Cliff Lee and Josh Hamilton. It's as simple as that. If these two put forth their best efforts, the Rangers play for the American League pennant. If not, then they continue their own post-season nine-game skid and their title hopes fade faster than manager Ron Washington's cocaine-trying phase.

Lee is a stud – capable of winning two games in each series. He is to Texas what Sabathia is to the Yankees – and he must win each game he starts. He is more than capable of doing so, even though he lost all three decisions against Tampa this year. He won consistently last year for Philadelphia, and can do it here.

Whether or not slugging outfielder Hamilton's fractured ribs are sufficiently healed, however, is an even bigger factor for the Rangers. With him, their line-up is formidable, including help from Vlad Guerrero, Nelson Cruz, and Ian Kinsler. Without him, it is only better than average, and no match for Tampa's young pitching staff. If Hamilton is unable to properly swing the bat, Texas' title hopes will wilt in the Arlington heat.

**Prediction: Rays in Four**

ALCS: The Championship Series, therefore, will be a matchup of AL East powers. In the end, the Rays' younger and more balanced pitching staff will emerge victorious over the Yankees, especially after Cy Young-hopeful David Price beats fellow candidate CC Sabathia in Game 1, placing the Yankees into a hole from which they cannot recover. That will be further magnified when either AJ Burnett or Javier Vasquez trots out to start a game, which will be tantamount to the Bronx Bombers waving the white flag in surrender.

**Prediction: Rays in Six**

And then it will be on to the World Series for Tampa, who will (like they did a couple of years ago) run into the steamroller from the City of Brotherly Love. The result? Phillies win it all. You heard it here first.

**Extra innings: One out of three (.333) isn't a bad batting average, but it is a dismal record when predicting the playoffs. The Yankees did sweep the Twins, but the Rangers beat the Rays in the other series and then steamrolled over the Yankees to gain entry into the World Series, where they lost to the San Francisco Giants. At least I knew that the National League winner would emerge triumphant.**

# Playoff Day 2 - an Ace, an Andy, and Anemia (October 8, 2010)

Baseball's run of great pitching continued last night, as the playoffs featured a freakishly amazing performance and saw two teams, riding stellar performances from their starting pitchers, take commanding leads over their hapless adversaries. The previous day had brought us a no-hitter from a playoff newcomer (Philadelphia's Roy Halladay) and a gem from the man who dominated the mound last post-season (Texas' Cliff Lee), and we wondered what the Giants' Tim Lincecum would do to match Halladay's and Lee's efforts.

*(writer's note – due to work, "back to school night", and a little-used commodity known as "sleep", I did not get to see more than one inning of each of the games yesterday. My recaps are based on what little I saw/listened to of the games themselves, as well as what I have read and heard both last night and this morning. I am aware of the fact that there were questionable calls in each game. I choose to ignore them here, though – if they didn't happen on the last play of the game, then the other team still had opportunities of their own. Let's not detract from the great performances)*

Nine innings. Two hits. One walk. Fourteen strikeouts. In his own post-season debut, the Giants' "Freak", Lincecum, came as close as possible to Halladay's Wednesday night gem. And he did so in as close a game as possible, which was won by the Giants by the slimmest of margins, 1-0. One could argue that his performance was as dominating, if not more, than Halladay's since the Phillies gave Doc an early lead – and that Lincecum was forced to pitch with more pressure throughout the game. Suffice it to say that it was clearly an incredible performance, one which overshadowed a great performance by the Braves' ace, Derek Lowe, and which evoked memories of the last game of the 1991 World Series, when Minnesota's Jack Morris out-dueled John Smoltz, throwing ten scoreless innings to give the Twins the championship over the same Atlanta Braves.

Meanwhile, in the American League, the Rays continued their inability to have bat meet ball, mustering only two hits against the Ranger's CJ Wilson and bullpen. Wilson was dominating for six plus innings, allowing only two hits, and wily veteran Darren Oliver shut Tampa down over two and a third hitless innings in relief. But Wilson is not Cliff Lee, and Oliver is no Mariano Rivera. The game also featured a home run from Texas' Michael Young, who, like Roy Halladay, had toiled in the majors for more than a decade before earning his first taste of October baseball. In only his second game, he made his presence known by putting the game out of reach with his three-run blast.

The Tampa bats are anemic. Losing two games at home by a combined score of 11-1 is no way to begin the playoffs, especially in a five-game series. They are traveling to Texas for Game 3, which really means nothing; because even if Tampa somehow rights its ship and pulls out a victory in that game, a rematch with the indomitable Cliff Lee looms in Game 4. The previous prediction must therefore be changed – give this round to Texas.

Andy Pettitte took the mound for the Yankees last night and extended his record for post-season wins, giving up two runs over seven innings in a 5-2 victory. Mariano Rivera pitched the ninth for the save, extending his post-season record for most saves ever by a reliever. The Yankees' win, in which they came back from an early 1-0 deficit against former New York hurler Carl Pavano, gave the Yankees a two-game lead in the best-of-five series.

<u>54-5</u>. Since the introduction of the five-game playoff series, 54 out of 59 teams that won the first two games eventually went on to capture those series. Both the Rangers and Yankees are currently sitting in that position, and both have the added luxury of having won both games on the road. They are both going home for two games in which they can dispose of their opposition, and both will again be throwing their aces, Cliff Lee for the Rangers, and CC Sabathia for the Yankees, in their respective Games 4. Lee has already shown that he can continue his magical post-season mastery. Sabathia will be out to prove that his performance in Game 1 was an anomaly, and that he can still be the post-season workhorse that he was in seasons past.

By the end of the weekend, there is little doubt that the AL Championship series will be set, and that the Yankees will be packing their bags for Texas. In the National League, if the first games are any indication, the maxim that pitching wins playoffs will continue, and there are two squads (Phillies and Giants) holding three aces. Each of their primary aces did their jobs in more than convincing fashion. Let's see if the others can follow suit.

**Extra innings: I was correct on all four counts. The Yankees and Phillies each went on to capture Game 3 and sweep their respective series. The Giants needed four games to vanquish the Braves, and the Rangers eventually ousted Tampa, winning their series in the full five games.**

**In that fifth game, Rangers' starter Cliff Lee threw a complete game, giving up only six hits and one run over his nine innings of work, during which he reaffirmed his post-season dominance by striking out eleven Rays. This was eerily reminiscent of his masterful Game 1 performance (seven innings, five hits, one run, and ten strikeouts) and led to the next post ...**

## Dear Joe: Throw ALCS Game 3 By Letting Burnett Pitch (October 13, 2010)

*Dear Mr. Girardi:*

*I presume that you watched the Rangers-Rays game last night. I assume that you watched Cliff Lee continue his run of post-season success, no doubt having at least a couple of flashbacks to the way that he dominated the Yankees in last year's World Series. And now you guys have to face his Rangers in the American League Championship Series. The only saving grace is that he will not pitch against you guys until Game 3.*

*Let's face some realities. Texas has some strong hitters, like Josh Hamilton and Vlad Guerrero. But the key to that team is Lee's pitching. That's why they got him, for his post-season success. Without boring you by reciting numbers that you already know, Mr. Lee is now 6-0 in his two-year post-season career. The only pitcher to start with more consecutive wins in the post-season was your old teammate, Orlando "El Duque" Hernandez. He is now the only pitcher to win two post-season games on the road in one series. And his post-season ERA is a microscopic 1.50 or so unheard of in today's baseball world The foregone conclusion, therefore, is that when he pitches, his team will win.*

*So you need to tank Game 3. Just let him win. You need to focus on the other games, so that the Yankees can win the series in five or six games and avoid the horrifying possibility of having to face Lee again in Game 7. Think about it - it is possible that the Yankees can be up 2-0, even though you are starting in Texas – no doubt your own post-season ace, CC Sabathia, has something to prove and will completely overpower the Rangers in Game 1. And based on Andy Pettitte's performance against Minnesota, he can spin his own post-season magic and win Game 2.*

*You have already announced that you will be using a four-man rotation in the ALCS, and that the enigmatic (is that a polite enough way of saying it?)*

*AJ Burnett will start at least one game. Conventional wisdom is that Phil Hughes will start Game 3 and Burnett will take the ball in Game 4. But that would be a mistake. Putting the young Hughes up against Cliff Lee is like the Romans throwing a Christian to the lions – simply not a fair fight. And we don't want to ruin Phil's psyche like that, especially if he is needed to pitch again in the series or, even better, in the World Series should the Yankees prevail.*

*No, the far better move is to let Burnett go out and lose to Lee. Realistically, he doesn't even merit a spot in the rotation based on his performance this year, and your "hopes" that he will regain his 2009 post-season form seem quite far-fetched. The man won a meager 10 games and lost 15 games this year - 15 losses on a team which was defeated only 65 times; that's almost a quarter of the team's losses. His ERA was well above 5, one of the highest for a starter in the Yankees' storied history, simply unacceptable for a playoff-caliber team, and his mental state is already shattered.*

*By the way, Joe, did he ever tell you where the mystery black eye came from? The public finds his evasiveness on the source of his black eye intriguing, so shouldn't you, as his manager, wonder the same? Not that it is important now, but it would be interesting to know. I initially thought he punched himself in a fit of anger, but now realize that could not be true - because if he had tried to aim and hit himself, then no doubt, like so many of his errant pitches this season, he would have missed.*

*So it's a win-win in the mental department. Either he loses (again) and simply continues his downward spiral, or he wins (by some miracle) and his mental state improves dramatically. It's a perfect scenario. Then, Hughes can pitch Game 4 in the Stadium, where he is most comfortable (I know, Game 3 is there also, but it's critical that he pitch there so you will not be giving this up), and the Yankees can take a commanding 3-1 series lead. Because mark my words, if you throw Hughes against Lee and Lee pitches the way that he has in the recent past, it's a guaranteed loss. And when Burnett then takes the mound for Game 4, it doesn't matter who throws for Texas - even if the Rangers exhume former Texas pitchers Rick Helling, Charlie Hough, or Ferguson Jenkins from the ranks of the retired, it will also be a guaranteed loss. At best, therefore, you would be tied 2-2. Why even allow that possibility?*

*The choice is clear. Burnett must be the sacrificial lamb in Game 3. That will cause the team the least pain and he has, through his lack of performance this year, certainly earned it. If he is a true team player, he will take this assignment like a man. It makes perfect sense.*

*Wish the team good luck in the Series; it's within their power to set up a World Series rematch with the Phillies.*

*And if you need any more advice, you know where to find me.*

*Sincerely yours,*

*Andrew Wolfenson*

*(on behalf of every Yankees' fan not named Burnett)*

**Extra innings:** **Mr. Girardi did not listen to my suggestion, as is explored in much greater depth later in this chapter.**

# Cablevision v. News Corp - Giants Winners, Viewers Losers (October 18, 2010)

Apparently Phillies' ace starting pitcher Roy Halladay isn't perfect. He, and his juggernaut of a team, can seemingly be beaten. They can be defeated, it appears, by a Florida castoff named Cody Ross, who allegedly touched "Doc" Halladay for two home runs in Game 1 of the NLCS, leading the Giants to victory. I use words like "apparently," "seemingly," and "allegedly" because I could not watch the game, as multi-million dollar corporations NewsCorp. and Cablevision, battling over what amounts to a few shekels to those entities, have conspired to temporarily delete FoxTV from the Cablevision lineup.

Or, it is possible that NewsCorp. simply pulled the station (and, here in the New York area, My9 as well), based on whether one believes the propaganda that Cablevision is currently running on those stations. Quite frankly, based on the allegations being hurled by each side, it is impossible to determine who is in the right; reports indicate that News Corp is seeking to have Cablevision pay up to $150 million per year for the right to include its stations on Cablevision, up from its current $70 million per year fee.

All that is known for certain is that Fox is not on the air for Cablevision subscribers.

Apparently last night the Phillies righted their ship, and rode Roy Oswalt's pitching and Jimmy Rollins' four RBI's to victory, evening their series with the Giants at one game apiece. I know this because I read it this morning on the internet.

My daughter is studying early 1900's history in school, and last night asked me if I knew what "Yellow Journalism" was. *"Of course,"* I answered, *"what do you think blogging is?"* Well, the majority of blogging, to be exact. Imagine what a great blogger William Randolph Hearst could have been.

91

Bloggers often write to legitimize their own position, and to inflame, no? And such *"yellow journalism"* it is also taking place right now on FoxTV; turn to Channel 5 and you are met with Cablevision's version of the events, how they are being stiff-armed by NewsCorp. into paying exorbitant fees to carry the station, and how they are attempting to protect our cable rates.

Is it true? The timing of the blackout, during the playoffs, would seem to imply that NewsCorp. is the heavy here. Then again, it is eerily reminiscent of last year's battle when Food Network was pulled off of Cablevision for several days. The mood in female-dominated households was dour for those two weeks. And at one point there was a battle with ABC, which also led to a temporary blackout. Perhaps the fact that history has repeated itself here signals that Cablevision is the heavy through its tactics. Hence the confusion.

Apparently the New York (really New Jersey) Football Giants beat the Detroit Lions yesterday by a 28-20 score. According to a radio report, it was a sloppy game by the G-Men, punctuated by eleven penalties. I can't say whether it was a sloppy game or not, because I was unable to watch the game due to the self-imposed Fox TV blackout. And in the 4:00 game, quarterback-cum-pervert Brett Favre and his Vikings defeated the Cowboys. Reports tell me that Dallas dominated the game. I cannot say whether it was a Cowboy-dominated game or not, because, as above, I could not watch the game on Fox because of the squabbles of two mega-corporations.

On a side note, I was euphoric on Saturday afternoon when I realized that the Yankees-Rangers game was to be televised on TBS, especially after the Yankees' amazing come-from-behind victory on Friday night. That euphoria lasted until the bottom of the first inning. Now, with the series also knotted at 1-1, the teams square off again tonight with Cliff Lee throwing for the Rangers. I have already set forth my complete fear of Mr. Lee, so while I hope the game is on TBS (I have not yet checked), at least if it is on Fox I will not have to watch him dominate the Bronx Bombers again.

The tally for the weekend, therefore, included two Giants' victories, one by the SF baseball team and one by the NY football team. And two other giants, through the airing of their dirty laundry and negotiating tactics, found themselves at an impasse where their viewers are the ones who are suffering.

I turned on the TV this morning, and still no Fox. As a result, we can only hope that this little brouhaha is resolved shortly, so that we can get back to the business of watching October baseball. And heaven help those companies if they have not resolved their issues by next Wednesday, when the *"Glee"* ode to *"The Rocky Horror Picture Show"* is scheduled to air. If Fox is not back on Cablevision by that time, thousands of households will be switching to FIOS just so they can watch *"Glee"*, because in this corporate battle, the viewers, sports fans and Gleeks alike, are the real losers. Until we take action of our own, that is.

## See Joe, I Told You So - But Am I Smiling? Sadly, No (October 20, 2010)

*That will be further magnified when either AJ Burnett or Javier Vasquez trots out to start a game, which will be tantamount to the Bronx Bombers waving the white flag in surrender.*

- Andy (the Oracle) Wolfenson, Oct. 6, 2010

*****

*Because mark my words, if you throw Hughes against Lee and Lee pitches the way that he has in the recent past, it's a guaranteed loss. And when Burnett then takes the mound for Game 4, it doesn't matter who throws for Texas - even if the Rangers exhume former Texas pitchers Rick Helling, Charlie Hough, or Ferguson Jenkins from the ranks of the retired, it will also be a guaranteed loss. At best, therefore, you would be tied 2-2. Why even allow that possibility?*

*The choice is clear. Burnett must be the sacrificial lamb in Game 3.*

- Andy (the Seer) Wolfenson, Oct. 13. 2010

*****

*Now, with the series also knotted at 1-1, the teams square off again tonight with Cliff Lee throwing for the Rangers. I have already set forth my complete fear of Mr. Lee, so while I hope the game is on TBS (I have not yet checked), at least if it is on Fox I will not have to watch him dominate the Bronx Bombers again.*

- Andy (the Know-it-All) Wolfenson, Oct. 18, 2010

94

How many times could I have said the same thing? How many people had to scream in the Yankee manager's ear to convince him that he was not using his starting rotation correctly against Texas and their superhuman playoff-stud pitcher? The choice was **clear-** if he was intent on using AJ Burnett, he had to be used against the Rangers' Cliff Lee in a proverbial "kill two birds with one stone" scenario.

Well, Yankee skipper Joe Girardi, perhaps trying to hasten his possible 2011 departure for the Windy City's North Side (*apparently he didn't see the news that the Cubs, possibly also questioning his managerial tactics, aborted their potential marriage to him and hired Mike Quade as manager yesterday afternoon*), did not listen to those who saw the reality of Mr. Burnett's *fait accompli* inefficiency. He did at least throw veteran Andy Pettitte against Mr. Lee in Game 3, but he still failed to realize the effect that Lee would have on the Yankees' hitters (terror? fear?), for the result was no different. Once Pettitte yielded a home run in the first inning, the game was, for all intents and purposes, over:

**Game 3: Rangers 8 – Yankees 0**

Cliff Lee: 8 innings, 2 hits, 1 walk, 0 runs, 13 strikeouts.

And then, as the follow-up last night:

**Game 4: Rangers 10 – Yankees 3**

AJ Burnett: 6 innings, 6 hits, 3 walks, 5 runs**

     \** including a back-breaking 3-run homer to Bengie Molina

In yesterday's fiasco, the newest version of "Clueless Joe" (*this is actually how at least one NY tabloid referred to Joe Torre, the previous Yankee manager and original "Joe-bot", when he was first hired by the Yankees)* let the enigmatic Burnett overstay his tenuous welcome on the mound and the Yankees again went down to a pre-destined defeat. Clearly, Burnett didn't lose the game by himself. Girardi never should have let him pitch to Molina at a time when the Rangers could have taken the lead, regardless of what his notebooks told him. The Yankee bats have been abysmal in the series, save the 8th inning of Game 1, so they are certainly also to blame. Mark Teixeira, he of the 0-for-ALCS batting performance, left the game (and the series) last night with what appears to be a pulled hamstring. The manager made bad decision after bad decision with his pitching staff, leading to the Rangers blowing another game wide open.

But in the end, the outcomes of Games 3 and 4 were both Yankee losses, as predicted so clearly by this writer and others.

So, to all of the naysayers out there, I was right. I was sadly, horribly, devastatingly, absolutely correct. I was 100% on the mark. And I was clearly not the only one who saw the need to sacrifice Burnett's start and to have him play Christian to Mr. Lee's Lion.

Now, the Yankees are buried, mired, and trapped in what is, seemingly, an insurmountable 3-1 deficit. To advance, they now have to win three straight games, including two in Texas and a Game 7 rematch between Messrs. Lee and Pettitte. It is simply not going to happen.

Apparently this year's World Series will take place, at least in part, in the Arlington heat. And maybe the Texas two-stepping celebration will start on the Yankee Stadium grass later today, if the demoralized and mis-managed Yankees don't pull themselves up out of the mire that their manager, poor pitching, and feeble hitting have wrought.

## Joe Girardi: Slave to Statistics, Maven of Match-ups (October 23, 2010)

**Pre-game notes: The Yankees did end up losing the playoff series to Texas, due, in large part, to some questionable actions by their manager. His handling of the pitching staff during the series drew ire from many pundits, and is the focus of this post.**

The pivotal moment in last night's ALCS game, the moment that ensured the Yankees an early ticket home to the Bronx for the off-season, was when manger Joe Girardi strode to the moment in the wake of Vlad Guerrero's two-run hit off of Phil Hughes. At that moment, Girardi (let's call him "Joe-bot"), in an effort to stop the Texas offense, was empowered and entrusted with choosing the best arm to keep New York's pennant hopes alive.

And he failed miserably, due to his ever-present and computer-like belief in match-ups and numbers. The "human element", as it were, never entered his mind. Recall the situation – Yankees down three games to two, needing a victory to force a decisive game 7. Yankee ace/horse CC Sabathia announced before the game that he would be available in relief if needed – and the New York mantra became the "all hands on deck" (the ability to use all pitchers, even other starting pitchers, if needed) mentality that is used when one is facing elimination.

The Yankees fell behind 3-1, and it was clear that Hughes was finished. Time to go to CC, right? Let him try to stop the Rangers in their tracks and give the dormant Yankee bats time to erupt before night's end. Wrong. Joe-bot instead brought in David Robertson, who, up until that point, had been nothing short of combustible (he had previously turned a 2-0 deficit in Game 3 into an 8-0 loss with his ineffectiveness on the mound). And true to form, the move backfired. The very next batter - Nelson Cruz – bang! Two-run homer, 5-1 deficit, and end of game, end of ALCS, end of season.

When asked afterward why he went to Robertson, Joe-bot offered the following explanation: *"I brought in a righty reliever. They had some righties coming up. I thought I would use CC against the lefties at the bottom of the lineup."*

There it is. Instead of bringing in his horse, he decided to bring in an inferior pitcher, to play the lefty-righty game that he fiddled with day-in-and-day-out all season. His notebook of charts and graphs told him to bring in the relatively inexperienced Robertson, who could barely get any batters out a couple of times, because he was born right-handed. Like the equally-mechanical Joe Torre before him, Girardi is a slave to his percentages, the lefty-righty idea often resulting in way too many pitching changes – like the game when Robertson actually did get two straight guys out but was lifted in favor of Boone Logan, touted as the lefty reliever assigned to face slugger Josh Hamilton – and Hamilton sent a laser out of the park. Robertson couldn't have done any worse, right?

But wait a minute, Mariano Rivera was also blessed to be a righty, and he is the greatest closer in post-season history. Why wouldn't Joe-bot bring Mariano in, if he was so concerned with a righty-righty situation? Nobody asked him that pointed question, but the answer is obvious – it wasn't the eighth inning yet – Mariano can't see the mound until the eighth or ninth because he is the closer. And to bring in a closer earlier in the game, to statistics and numbers junkies like Joe-bot, is sacreligious.

Of course it is possible that if Sabathia had been brought in, he would have given up hits or runs due to his relative ineffectiveness in the past two starts. But, like above, he couldn't have done any worse, right? And if Girardi, eschewing his charts, graphs, and figures, had gone to Sabathia, and had Sabathia let the team down through giving up runs, etc., it would have been infinitely easier to explain and accept. I would not be writing this blog if Sabathia had come in and surrendered the home run to Cruz. Because bringing in Sabathia would have been true to the "all hands on deck" concept – not simply keeping to his playbook, his overwhelming urge to keep playing percentage baseball, forgetting any human element to the process and, most importantly, forgetting that, for his team, there was no tomorrow.

This doesn't even take into account the questionable nature of intentionally walking Josh Hamilton for a second time in order to have Hughes face Vlad Guerrero. It's not like Guerrero was a kid, or incapable of delivering a big hit. Perhaps if he had simply let Hughes face Hamilton, he could have gotten him out and the inning would have ended 1-1. The main reason for the loss was the Yankees' inability to hit; but taking them out of the game through bonehead pitching machinations did not help give them any opportunity to change their fortunes. If anything, it made the hitters press more and led to greater failure.

At least now Joe-bot will have six full months to contemplate his next pitching change. Maybe, with that much time to prepare, he will not screw it up. Then again, it depends on what the notebooks say …

# FIFTH INNING

## OTHER YANKEE-RELATED BLOGS

Not surprisingly, the majority of blogs that I have written over the past few years have focused on the Yankees, the team that I have followed since I first discovered baseball (and the team's rich history) as a young boy. Several of the posts have been put into other sections of the book (Alex Rodriguez and Mariano Rivera each have their own chapters/innings, for example, and the prior chapter/inning dealt with the Playoffs and World Series) – so this inning contains the "other" Yankee blogs, those which did not fit into the other delineated categories.

*The kids at a Yankee game (2008) – and wearing their favorite player's number*

# The Yankees - New York's Kings of November (November 17, 2009)

17 days into the new month, the Yankees have retained their status as sports kings of the Big Apple, even as the baseball season has become but a fond (or not so fond) memory for most. Their last victory was two weeks ago, yet it remains fresh in our memories not only for the fact that it closed out the World Series or because it returned the coveted trophy to the Bronx.

Rather, the Yankees' November 4, game six win stands, somewhat remarkably, as the last victory to be celebrated by a New York area professional team in the "big three" sports – baseball, football, and basketball. Moreover, and equally improbably, the Yankees, playing in a sport which is to extend only through October, currently, on the 17th day of November, have more November victories than **any** of the remaining New York sports teams. In fact, they have more November victories than all of the remaining New York sports teams **combined**! Because over the past thirteen days, there have been no victories for any of the New York teams.

A little further research reveals that as of today – the 17*th*, count 'em, 17*th* day of November - the victory tally for the greater New York area stands as follows:

Yankees – two victories
Giants – no victories
Jets – no victories
Knicks – one victory
Nets – no victories

Even extending our scope to the only football team that actually plays in New York (as famously pointed out by then-Governor Mario Cuomo), the

101

answer remains the same, because the Buffalo Bills are similarly winless since the calendar page turned to November.

November's tally therefore reveals a tie: Yankee reliever Joba Chamberlain - one victory; The Giants, Jets, Bills, Knicks, and Nets – *combined* - one victory. Start that fist-pumping, Joba, you are tied for first!

To put this in further perspective, this means that newly-elected Governor Chris Christie has more November victories in the Garden State (one) than the Giants, Jets, and Nets combined. And to return to the gridiron, the woeful St. Louis Rams and Tampa Bay Buccaneers, who are a combined two-for-2009, have tasted victory more times in November than the five teams currently representing, and I use the term loosely, New York and New Jersey in the NFL and NBA, combined.

So for now, the pinstriped phenoms reign as New York's November champions. But nothing is forever. Sadly, the Yankees' stranglehold on the "W" column will likely come to an end on Saturday when the Knicks play the Nets in the 2009 *"Battle of Hardwood Ineptitude"*. As such, even if both teams lose their remaining games leading up to this "Clash of the (non) Titans", one must, by definition, emerge victorious on Saturday. Then again, if any two teams could play to a tie, it would be them - so anything is possible.

**Extra innings:** **The Jets eventually won nine games in the 2009 season, capturing one more victory than the Giants, who finished 8-8. The Jets then won two additional games in the playoffs, losing to the Indianapolis Colts in the AFC Championship game. The two basketball teams limped to the finish of the 2002-2010 season; the Knicks only won 29 games all season, and the Nets, continuing their November ineptitude, finished dead last in the entire NBA with 12 victories.**

# Memories of a Home Run - Marcus and Me (February 10, 2010)

Our memories are, to a large extent, what make us who we are. Certain memories, of course, resonate greater than others. Milan Kundera wrote that the memory of revulsion is greater than the memory of happiness. We can recall in great detail the horrible events of our lives, especially those events which had great societal impact. Any person over the age of 50 can likely recount the circumstances under which they heard of President Kennedy's death. I can vividly describe the details of when I heard of such public tragedies as the death of Thurman Munson, the shooting of John Lennon, the Challenger explosion, and the horrible events of 9/11. The memories are so clear and vivid, it is as if they all took place yesterday.

There are many good memories as well; personal memories such as my wedding day, the births of my children, finding out I had passed the Bar exam, winning my first jury trial, etc. There were the "brushes with greatness" – the interviews that I was fortunate enough to conduct while with my school newspaper – members of the Philadelphia 76ers, the then-unknown rock band "Poison", political satirist Mark Russell, boxer Gerry Cooney, and baseball commissioner Bart Giamatti.

I also have also vivid recollections of more global events; and many of those are rooted in sports: watching the 1980 Olympic hockey team beat the Russians; watching the Yankees reach the World Series on Chris Chambliss' last-inning home run all those years ago; watching the Giants win their first Super Bowl over two decades ago.

But the best sports memories are those witnessed live. I have been in Yankee Stadium for the good, such as playoff and World Series victories, including the "Jeffrey Maier" game, and the bad, like the 22-4 shellacking at the hands of the Indians shortly after the opening of the new Stadium last year. In

Oakland, I attended the first major league game pitched by Barry Zito, then touted as a pitcher who could become the best ever. In Anaheim, I sat and watched the Red Sox' Dustin Pedroia step onto a major league field for, according to the Sox fan seated alongside me, the first time.

And perhaps the obscure memories are the best of all. Any person who has sat in the stands during a perfect game, witnessed record-breaking home runs, or had the pleasure of watching the sports' elite bestow gift upon gift to the fans with their remarkable play, can speak of those moments for their entire lives with great reverence. Other fans will listen to the tales and wish that they, too, had been there that day. Some people claim to have borne witness to certain events, even though they had not. It has been said that there were perhaps a couple of thousand people in the Hershey, PA arena the day that Wilt Chamberlain scored his record 100 points in one game. Thereafter, however, hundreds of thousands claimed to have been there. As Dire Straits' Mark Knopfler once sang, *"Two men say they're Jesus. One of them must be wrong"*. The same is often true of famous, or record-setting, events.

The obscure, however, conjures up an entirely different emotion. Not one of jealousy, but maybe simple recognition that the speaker was present for something special, even if the annals of sport do not recount that event in any more than hushed tones.

This week, the Yankees signed Marcus Thames to a minor-league contract, bringing back a player who spent the initial part of his major league career in pinstripes; a nondescript career, to say the least, with one notable exception. On June 10, 2002, the Arizona Diamondbacks came to face the Yankees in a rematch of the prior year's World Series. Pitching for Arizona was Randy Johnson, arguably the greatest pitcher of the last decade and a certain future Hall of Famer. That day, Marcus Thames was making his major league debut.

On the first pitch he saw from Johnson, the first pitch that he saw as a major leaguer, Thames launched a home run, becoming only the 80th person in baseball history to hit a home run in his first at-bat. A curtain call followed, tipping his cap to the roaring Yankee Stadium crowd, which would signal the high point of his first tour with the Yankees.

And I was there. I remember it like it was yesterday. Every time the name Marcus Thames has been mentioned over the past eight years, I have thought of that home run. And every time I think of it, I smile. It is a moment of relative obscurity, no doubt, but one that I never hesitate to recount whenever Mr. Thames' name is evoked.

**Extra innings: Interestingly, Thames also hit a home run in his first at-bat as a member of the Texas Rangers, to whom he was traded by the Yankees in 2003. He is now retired, having seen his last major-league action in 2011 as a member of the Los Angeles Dodgers. Over a ten-year career, he donned four different uniforms (Yankees, Rangers, Tigers, Dodgers) and slugged 115 home runs, but none as special as the first one.**

**As noted above, he was the 80th player in baseball history to hit a home run in his first at-bat. He was also the second of only three men to have done it while wearing a Yankees' uniform, with the others being John Miller (Sept. 11, 1966) and Andy Phillips (Sept. 26, 2004).**

**Since Thames' heroics, 34 other players have homered in their first at-bat, meaning that the exclusive club has now swollen to 114. And Met fans can take special pride in this club, as their four members (Benny Ayala, Mike Fitzgerald, Kazuo Matsui, and Mike Jacobs) give them more members than the Yankees. The last player to join the club was Jurickson Profar of the Texas Rangers, on September 2, 2012.**

# Red $ox $igning$ $end Yankee$ to Take De$perate Mea$ure$ (December 9, 2010)

La$t night, the Bo$ton Red $ox' owner$ opened their wallet$ for the $econd time thi$ off-$ea$on and threw million$ of dollar$ at free-agent outfielder Carl Crawford. The effect$ of thi$ $igning were far-reaching acro$$ the ba$eball $trato$phere, and have led to a $ituation where the major$' highe$t $alaried team is de$perately $eeking way$ to $qua$h their arch-enemy'$ newly-$igned $uper$tar$.

Within the pa$t week, the $ox have traded for (and then $igned to a mega-contract) $an Diego $lugger Adrian Gonzalez and $igned Crawford, thereby e$tabli$hing them$elve$ a$ the $tudlie$t team in the American League. Bo$ton now po$$e$$e$ the be$t $tarting lineup and the be$t $tarting rotation in the league, and, reali$tically, anything le$$ than a World $erie$ championship thi$ $ea$on $hould be con$idered a cola$$al failure, the bigge$t in Ma$$achu$ett$ $ince John Kerry'$ failed run for Pre$ident.

In re$pon$e to Bo$ton'$ $hopping $pree, the Yankee$ have reportedly increa$ed their offer to the cla$$ of thi$ year'$ free agent pitcher$, Cliff Lee, to $even year$. A$$uming that the offer i$ in the $ame general area a$ their prior $ix-year offer, that mean$ that the offer exceed$ $150 million or $o. Thi$ i$ $taggering, and i$ nothing $hort of ludicrou$. A $even-year contract for a pitcher who ha$ a recent hi$tory of back trouble$? A$ Yankee legend Yogi Berra $aid: "it'$ deja vu all over again" - who remember$ Kevin Brown? Clearly, the current Yankee bra$$ doe$ not. He also $igned a hundred million dollar plu$ contract, for $even year$, had a bad back, and then, like the other overpaid albatro$$e$ of year$ pa$t, imploded following hi$ trade to the Yankee$ during the 2003 off-$ea$on. The $ame could ea$ily happen here.

$imply put, the Yankee$ are in de$peration mode. I can $mell their de$peration from acro$$ the GW Bridge, and can even $en$e it from all the way down $outh in their $ea$onal home ba$e in Tampa. They are $uddenly running $cared, and $omehow $eem to believe that the only way to $alvage this $ea$on is to $ign Lee, no matter what the co$t.

$everal year$ ago, Red $ox owner John Henry called the Yankee$ the "Evil Empire". For year$, Red $ox fan$ have complained that the Yankee$ $imply out$pent every other team, which wa$ why they were more $ucce$$ful. What are the $ox fan$ going to $ay now if they don't $weep their way to $erie$ glory?

$ome might $ee thi$ as the petty jealou$y of a Yankee$ fan. Not true. The money being thrown at the$e player$, by both team$, is $imply ridiculou$. The economy i$ in the toilet. $20M plus per year for any of the$e player$ is $imply too much - it i$ too much for Crawford, and it i$ too much for Lee. The $ame i$ al$o true for the $miling face of the Yankee$ franchi$e, $hort$top Derek Jeter - he didn't de$erve $17M per $ea$on, other than for hi$ marketing prowe$$.

Perhap$ the owner$ of these two team$ will take a few $tep$ back and curb the $pending a bit, e$pecially when neither win$ the champion$hip thi$ year.

$eriou$ly? Of cour$e not. They will keep on $helling out million$ of dollar$ and di$tancing them$elve$ from the re$t of the team$. In their mind$, that i$. Becau$e the Yankee$, with their $tarting lineup including $everal member$ of the 35 and older crowd, won't be able to keep pace with the young$ter$ who $erve on team$ like Tampa Bay. And the Yankee pitcher$, even if they $ign Lee, will $till be compri$ed of CC $abathia and a bunch of guy$ with bad back$ or bad head$.

And the $ox? They will $ee, the hard way, that $imply $pending hundred$ of million$ of dollar$ a $ea$on doe$ not a$$ure a team of winning a champion$hip. Million$ of dollar$ doe$ not guarantee $ucce$$ or, more importantly, team chemi$try. La$t $ea$on $aw the Giant$ be$t the Ranger$ in the Fall Cla$$ic. Neither of tho$e team$ were among the league$' bigge$t $pender$.

It'$ going to be a long, hot $ummer. E$pecially for two team$ who$e inflated payroll$ will, quite po$$ibly, not tran$late to $ucce$$ on the field.

**Extra innings: Boston's signings, to say the least, were unsuccessful. The team has failed to make the post-season since making the moves to obtain Gonzalez and sign Crawford. Last year, in the midst of a season marked by dissension and on-and-off the field difficulties, both Gonzalez and Crawford were sent to the Los Angeles Dodgers.**

**The reality is that trying to "buy" a championship, more often than not, fails. This was again proven last season by the Miami Marlins, who opened their wallets and bought three high-priced free agents and opened a new ballpark with visions of competing for playoff glory. The team stumbled from the beginning of the season, however, and finished tied with the afore-mentioned Red Sox for the 24th most wins in the majors – meaning that only five teams had less victories. Similar to Boston, the Marlins also purged itself of the large salaries, making several off-season deals in which all three of the high-priced free agents, including shortstop Jose Reyes, were sent packing.**

**Yet, baseball teams continue to lavish large salaries on players who are middling at best. The Yankees rewarded Phil Hughes with a $7 million contract this off-season. Hughes did win 16 games for the Yankees last year, but his ERA was an inflated 4.23 and, only one year ago, he finished with a 5-5 record after being limited to 14 starts due to continued back problems.**

Middle relievers command salaries of millions of dollars per year, even those who considered "specialists" and who are often brought in to face one or two hitters. The salary structure has spiraled out of control, and owners have shown little signs of trying to harness their wallets. The Dodgers have joined the ranks of the free-spenders, and have amassed a mini-All-Star team of their own for 2013. Will this translate to postseason success? History would seem to dictate to the contrary.

And on those occasions when owners do try to show fiscal responsibility, they face criticism. Last year, the Angels' Mike Trout had one of the best, if not the best, rookie seasons in Major League history. Despite not being called up to the Angels until late April, he led the American League in both stolen bases and runs scored, and was the first player in Major League history to have at least 30 home runs, 45 stolen bases, and 125 runs scored in a season. He finished second in the MVP voting to Miguel Cabrera, and was a unanimous selection as Rookie of the Year. He accomplished all of that while earning $480,000.

For the 2013 season, the Angels increased his salary to $510,000, only $20,000 above the league minimum. Trout did not complain, but his agent, Craig Landis, whined that the renewal "falls well short of a 'fair' contract." Perhaps that is true, considering the record-setting season that Trout put together in 2012. Then again, he has only one year of experience, and it is possible that he may fall into a sophomore slump. More importantly, however, is that the Angels did not do anything wrong by renewing the contract for this amount. If Trout continues to produce, then when he is eligible for arbitration and free agency, then he will see his paydays.

And if he does sign a nine-figure contract at some point in the future, what if his production then wanes? What if, in the third year of a multi-year deal which brings him more than $20 million annually, his production suddenly drops? Will Craig Landis be speaking of "fairness" then? Likely not.

109

In an early 2013 interview with *The Wall Street Journal*, the Yankees' Mark Teixeira actually admitted that he was not worth the $20 million dollars that the Yankees pay him pursuant to his long-term contract. Invoking Trout's name, Teixeira was quoted as saying the following: *"[a]gents are probably going to hate me for saying it. You're not very valuable when you're making $20 million. When you're Mike Trout, making the minimum, you are crazy valuable. My first six years, before I was a free agent, I was very valuable. But there's nothing you can do that can justify a $20 million contract."*

Teixeira did not, however, offer to restructure his contract for less money or offer to give any of the money back to the team. No players have done so, despite the fact that many players (ahem, Alex Rodriguez) have shown dramatically lower production in the latter years of their blockbuster, long-term contracts.

And yet, the owners still offer such contracts. Witness the Free Agent class of 2013: Josh Hamilton – Angels (5 years, $125 million); Michael Bourn – Indians (4 years, $48 million); B.J. Upton - Braves (5 years, $75 million); Nick Swisher - Indians (4 years, $56 million); Angel Pagan - Giants (4 years, $40 million) – the bet here is that at all four of those teams will have some form of "buyer's remorse" before the contract terms are up. Note that the Indians may be satisfied with Bourn's production, but four years of Swisher will no doubt prove to be too much for the Cleveland faithful.

# Today is Baseball's Real Opening Day - The Yanks Begin Today (April 6, 2012)

**Pre-game notes: The beginning of this post was written completely tongue-in-cheek.**

Today is Opening Day. The real Opening Day. At 3:10 this afternoon, when Tampa's James Shields completes his warmup tosses and the first Yankee batter steps up to the plate, the 2012 baseball season will have officially begun. Forget about the games from yesterday or the alleged "opening night" game between St. Louis and Miami. Pay no mind to the two-game mini-series that took place in Japan last week between Oakland and Seattle. The baseball season does not officially start until the Yankees begin their first game.

It is time for all to admit that Major League Baseball, for better or for worse, still revolves around the Yankees, the greatest franchise ever to step onto a diamond. 27 World Championships, in and of themselves, establish the Bronx Bombers as the most successful professional sports team in this country, and the Yankees continue to dominate headlines even when they are not sitting atop baseball's standings.

These are certainly not the "Bronx Zoo" Yankees of the late 1970's. That team made headlines for reasons other than their play on the field, and often did so in ways that were embarrassing to the players and ownership – a televised, dugout fight between manager Billy Martin and star outfielder Reggie Jackson was the pinnacle (or nadir, depending on how you perceive it) of that era, along with Reggie's proclamation that he was the "straw that stirs the drink", a blatant dig at then-Captain Thurman Munson, and the seemingly never-ending cycle of owner/"Boss" George Steinbrenner hiring and firing (five times) the alcoholic, "Yankee for life" manager, Billy Martin. In contrast, this

111

team seems to make news by doing nothing, by going about its job in a business-like manner and allowing others to speak ill of them.

Bobby Valentine proved that this Spring, when the new Red Sox manager attempted to goad a response from his team's arch-rivals by picking on Derek Jeter and Alex Rodriguez. The responses from Jeter and A-Rod, however, were so minimal that news teams could not even fashion a real story about them. Perhaps Bobby V should be focusing on his own team, rather than his opposition. Even an excellent post about the Mets and their inadvertent benefactor/albatross, Bernie Madoff, took pains to compare the cranky writer's beloved Mets, in an unfavorable light, to the Yankees. Simply put, the Yankees are in everyone's minds. That's just the way that it is.

Thus concludes the arrogant, Yankees' fan post that everyone was expecting.

The reality is that this season brings many doubts, along with a great deal of intrigue and, possibly, sentiment, for the Yankees and their faithful. This may be the final year for the best closer ever to wear pinstripes (or any uniform), Mariano Rivera. The team is old. Questions abound about how Andy Pettitte will fare in his comeback. The team traded its best prospect for a seemingly sure-fire pitching ace, only to see that pitcher, Michael Pineda, begin the season on the disabled list with tendonitis in his shoulder. Alex Rodriguez has six years and about a zillion dollars left on his contract, and cannot seem to stay healthy. Relief pitcher and poster child for unfulfilled potential Joba Chamberlain suffered a compound fracture of his ankle in a freak trampoline accident during spring training.

The main issue, of course, is age. The Yankees are the oldest team in the majors, with an average age of 31 years, 222 days. This is almost a full year older than the geriatric squad whom many are picking to face them in the World Series, the almost 31-year old average Philadelphia Phillies. Rivera is 42. Pettitte is 40. The new DH, Raul Ibanez, is 39. New starting pitcher Hiroki

Kuroda is 37. Jeter is 37, and Rodriguez is 36. They are old. Staying injury-free may be the biggest challenge that this team faces this year.

Luckily for the men from the Bronx, none of the other teams in the American League's Eastern Division did much to improve themselves over this off-season. The biggest change for the rival Red Sox, aside from bringing in the fiery Valentine as manager, was to lose their closer (to the Phillies) and bring in a new fireman, Andrew Bailey, who will miss at least half of the season to a thumb injury. The Rays brought back Carlos Pena to play first base and the Blue Jays have rising star Brett Lawrie, but none of these teams, on paper, can stand up to New York's squad.

So yes, the 2012 baseball season really starts today. A 162-game race which will be run, in the Bronx, by a group of men, nine to be exact, who were born before or during the "Bronx Zoo" heyday of their 1970's predecessors. With Pettitte's return, three of the "core four" who led the team to championships in the late 1990's and 2000 are still around to show the young boys how to play, and how to win. And perhaps they will win the title again this year.

Already many are predicting the Yankees to advance to the World Series, where they will either lose to or defeat (depending on which predictions you are reading) the Phillies. But whether or not they make the Series, or even the playoffs, you will be reading about them. You will be hearing about them. They are firmly entrenched in the baseball nation's collective psyche. And there is nothing you can do about it.

**Extra innings: Neither the Yankees nor Phillies made it to the World Series last year. In fact, while the Yankees' collapse in the playoffs was demoralizing (being swept by Detroit), the Phillies were, arguably, the most under-performing team of the 2012 campaign as they finished with a record**

113

of 81-81, finishing third in the National League Eastern Division, 17 games behind the upstart Washington Nationals.

It was actually worse in Boston, where the afore-mentioned manager Bobby Valentine alienated his players, especially those veterans who had been key members of the prior World Series championship team. Some of those players allegedly went behind his back to complain about him to team ownership. Popular third baseman Kevin Youkilis was sent packing mid-season to the White Sox following the player revolt, and the Sox limped to season's end with a clearly lame-duck manager. Valentine was officially fired following the end of the season, but rumors abounded that he had previously cut a deal with ownership, months earlier, and that he had not been fired mid-season only to spare him and the team from additional embarrassment.

# A Tale (Tail) of Two D.J.'s - An Anniversary and A Birthday (June 1, 2012)

Twenty years ago, the Yankees drafted the player who would become the cornerstone of their franchise, the man who would be a key cog in their return to World Series glory, and the only man to amass 3,000 hits while wearing pinstripes. On June 1, 1992, the Yankees drafted their future Captain, perennial All-Star, five-time World Series champion, and future Hall of Famer Derek Jeter.

Perhaps it is fitting, therefore, that his namesake, my son, celebrates his fifth birthday today.

**Happy Birthday, DJ, you wear the name well.**

*My boy coming home for the first time (note the Yankees' shirt)*

*In his own Derek Jeter jersey*

**Extra innings:** The date is a complete coincidence, by the way. Luckily for us, DJ is much like Derek Jeter – loved by all. We like to think that he brings honor to the name – with perhaps one exception. Despite the fact that his name really is "DJ", some people still want to believe that his real name is "Derek Jeter" – which led to one time at the vet's office when one of the staff called out, rather loudly, in search of the results of "Derek Jeter's stool sample" – causing many curious heads to turn.

# Mr. October's July Hit - Reggie Jackson Questions A-Roid (July 10, 2012)

In the late 1970's, outspoken right fielder and designated hitter Reggie Jackson was one of the main cogs of the "Bronx Zoo" New York Yankees. Without a doubt, he was the most quotable member of that team, a squad known not only for its back-to-back World Series titles in 1977 and 1978 but also for its internal strife, clubhouse antics, and the managerial merry-go-round which featured Reggie-hater and alcoholic Billy Martin. Reggie burst onto the New York scene following a successful career in Oakland, signing for almost three million dollars, up until that point one of the biggest free agent contracts in baseball history.

Jackson caused controversy immediately upon his arrival in the Big Apple, being quoted in a *Sport* Magazine article that he would be the most important member and leader on the Yankees, a role that, in his mind, could not be properly filled by then Yankee-captain Thurman Munson.

*"This team, it all flows from me. I'm the straw that stirs the drink. Maybe I should say me and Munson, but he can only stir it bad."*

The comment, of course, caused great acrimony between Jackson and Munson, the reigning American League Most Valuable Player and Yankee catcher. Ostracized by many in the Yankee clubhouse, Reggie publically spoke about the difficulties in being an articulate black man, and raised issues about what he (correctly) perceived to be manager Billy Martin's racial bias.

Following a nationally televised battle between Martin and Jackson in the Fenway Park dugout, the team began to gel and reached the World Series in 1977 – and it was there that Jackson turned the Fall Classic into his own personal stage, belting three home runs in the final game of the series to clinch the championship for the Yankees and return the World Series trophy to the Bronx for the first time since the early 1960's. It was then that he earned the

117

nickname "Mr. October", which was coined, likely not in a friendly way, by Munson.

*"If I played in New York, they would name a candy bar after me."*

And they did. The *"Reggie Bar"* was introduced after Jackson began playing with the Yankees. On Opening Day 1978, the Yankees had a *"Reggie Bar"* giveaway. Jackson homered in that game, and bars rained from the stands onto the field in celebration. Jackson left New York as a free agent after the 1981 season, reportedly bitter that the Yankees had made no efforts at re-signing him. Yankee owner George Steinbrenner later said that allowing Jackson to leave was the biggest mistake that he had made during his ownership of the Yankees, and Jackson was brought back into the Yankee family, as a special advisor, in 1993.

*"I didn't come to New York to be a star, I brought my star with me."*

The timing of this hiring was intriguing to many in light of the fact that Jackson was to be inducted into the Hall of Fame in 1993. Jackson's plaque shows him wearing the familiar interlocking N-Y Yankee cap, which many believed was bought by Steinbrenner through the hiring. It was said that he should have worn an Oakland hat, having begun his career and after his success with the A's, but Jackson chose to wear the Yankee hat – it should be noted that players no longer determine which hat they wear on their plaque. It is determined by the Hall of Fame Committee.

Flash forward to 2012, and outspoken Yankee employee Reggie Jackson is at it again, stirring the pot for the now-corporate and boring New York Yankees. Referring to current outspoken Yankee slugger Alex Rodriguez, who has admitted to the use of performance-enhancing drug usage in the past, Jackson had this to say:

*"... I think there are real questions about his numbers. As much as I like him, what he admitted about his usage does cloud some of his records."*

Jackson retired from major league baseball with 563 home runs, which at the time was sixth on the all-time homer list. He has since watched a parade of steroid-enhanced monsters power their way past him on the list, including Sammy Sosa, Rodriguez, Mark McGwire, Rafael Palmeiro, and the current (with an asterisk) home run king, Barry Bonds. So is Jackson bitter? It is likely. But nothing with Reggie is that simple; from his early playing days until today, he has been a complex case study, a man with a claimed IQ of 160, a man who often had difficulty keeping his emotion in check and who became a lightning rod for racial politics and outspoken critic of many.

Former teammate Mickey Rivers once summed up Jackson, whose full name was Reginald Martinez Jackson: *"No wonder you're mixed up. You've got a white man's first name, a Spanish man's middle name, and a black man's last name."*

Was Jackson wrong in his assessment of Rodriguez? Absolutely not. Due to this admission of steroid use, it is fair to state that Rodriguez's numbers will be forever questioned. That is why the response was lukewarm when he recently slammed career grand slam homer number 23, tying all-time Yankee great Lou Gehrig for the major league record. Nobody from the steroid era, who has admitted to use or who has been suspected of such use, has yet been permitted to enter the Hall of Fame. McGwire, Sosa, Palmeiro, Bonds, et al thought that they had stamped their ticket to Cooperstown through their exploits on the field; to date, however, the voters have denied them such induction. Why should Rodriguez be any different?

Reports out of Yankee camp are that Reggie has now been asked to stay away from the team for a period of time, seemingly to avoid the distraction that his presence would cause Rodriguez and his teammates. For the now

119

corporate-minded Yankees, it makes at least a modicum of sense; but when contrasted with the "Bronx Zoo" Yankees, and Jackson, who constantly stirred not only the drink, but also the pot, it seems ridiculous. Perhaps it was improper of Jackson to question Rodriguez, but only because he is currently employed by the Yankees. But the "punishment", to the extent that it should have been handed down, should have been limited to an apology, not a de facto suspension.

Jackson deserves better. He can fill an entire hand with World Series rings, having won three titles with Oakland (1972 – 1974) and two with New York (1977 – 1978). Rodriguez boasts one such ring. Jackson clubbed 563 non-steroid assisted home runs. Rodriguez has over 600, but, as noted by Reggie, the amount is clouded by his steroid use. Reggie was the biggest star on his team, perhaps to the chagrin of the other late-70's Yankees. Rodriguez has been forced, often much to his chagrin, to toil in the shadow of Derek Jeter. Simply put, Jackson is more important to the Yankees.

*"The only difference between me and those other great Yankees is my skin color."*

Rodriguez could have been more important; and perhaps that is why the ownership took action against Jackson. Rodriguez is in the middle of a long-term deal with the club, one that still has five years remaining. There is no doubt that the Yankee brass is now kicking themselves over the time, and multi-millions of dollars, remaining on that deal. When the deal was signed, the expectation was that Rodriguez would eventually break baseball's immortal slugging records. He would hit enough home runs to pass Bonds on the all-time list, and, more importantly, he would do so in pinstripes and bring the crown back to New York, where it has not resided since Hank Aaron passed Babe Ruth in 1974.

The Yankees did not, however, foresee that Rodriguez would admit to use of steroids shortly thereafter. Nor did they foresee the erosion of his skills, to the point where he is now little more than an average third baseman. Any delusions of him becoming the Home Run King have vanished, and, instead, the Yankees are now saddled with his long, and expensive contract. So it is imperative, apparently, for them to keep their aging albatross content, to keep distraction away from him, and hope that he can, in some measure, justify the $30 million dollars per year that the team is paying him.

But keeping Jackson away is not the answer. He is a link to the team's colorful past, a man who helped bring the championship trophy back to the Bronx, and a man who, as the ownership must be aware, is not afraid to speak his mind.

*"After Jackie Robinson the most important black in baseball history is Reggie Jackson, I really mean that."*

No doubt he believes it. The Yankees would be well-served to continue to honor him for his accomplishments on the field. One comment, echoing public sentiment about a self-admitted steroid user, cannot serve to change that.

**Extra innings: Jackson's comments appear to take on greater validity based on the most recent PED allegations facing Rodriguez, allegations which Rodriguez has yet to properly address because he is, as he has said, "100%" committed to his rehabilitation efforts. The Yankees, meanwhile, appear to be taking great pains to distance themselves from Rodriguez – he is currently rehabilitating from off-season his surgery, but rather than have him do so with the team in Tampa, he is undergoing such rehab in New York. The likelihood is that these positions will flip once the calendar turns to April. When the Yankees return north for the beginning of the 2013 season, it will not be a surprise to see A-Rod take his rehab sessions to Tampa.**

## Yankees Mauled - Now it is Time to Rip Them to Shreds (October 22, 2012)

The World Series begins this week, and for what seems to be the umpteenth year in a row to a frustrated Yankee nation, it will be conducted without the presence of the highest-paid team in the majors, the New York Yankees. Tonight's NL Championship Series Game 7 will decide the Tigers' opponent for the championship, and the cats from Detroit will need to be reminded that, whether they are facing the Cardinals or Giants, their next opponents will put up much more of a fight than the sputtering Yankees did last week.

Simply put, the Tigers mauled the Yankees. The teams played four games. The teams played 39 innings. In those 39 innings, the Yankees scored but six runs. Take away a four-run outburst in the ninth inning of Game 1, and the allegedly-mighty Bronx Bombers tallied two runs in 37 innings – one of them coming on an Eduardo Nunez (yes, Eduardo Nunez) home run and the other coming when Nunez (yes, the same guy) scored after he tripled in Game 4. Clearly, the anemic offensive display put on by the vaunted Yankees' lineup left much to be desired. The Tigers simply cannot expect either San Francisco or St. Louis to roll over and die as easily.

And what of the Yankees, you may ask. In what direction will this team of aging stars go in 2013? Clearly, the lineup must be changed. Anything less than a World Series victory is, famously, unacceptable to the Steinbrenner regime. The only real question is where to change the lineup.

The popular rally cry now is to rid the Yankees of 58-year-old Alex Rodriguez – but, bucking conventional wisdom, this writer disagrees. I disagree based on the following three numbers: **$114,000,000**      **14**      **99**

The first number, of course, is the monies that the Yankees owe A-Rod over the remaining life of his contract, which will take him into his early 60s. If they are simply going to pay the bulk of these monies to have him wear someone else's uniform, then they should just keep him here and reap the benefits (cough) of his mediocre performances over the next five years. But that alone is not reason to keep him. The reason why he will stay in pinstripes is the Yankees' love of publicity and presence in the record books. Why was Lightning-Rod signed to such a long and extravagant contract extension years ago? One simple reason – so that he could pass Barry Bonds and bring the career home run title back to New York, where it rightfully belongs – back to the House that sits across the street from the House that Ruth Built – so that Babe Ruth's once seemingly unassailable home run record could once again "come home" to roost in the Bronx.

That was, of course, before his revelation of prior steroid use and a seemingly incomprehensible diminution of his talent – except that the two go together, don't they? He is a shadow of his former self, and clearly not worth his contract. His statistics are tainted, like those of Bonds, Sosa, Palmeiro and McGwire before him.

Despite the taint that will accompany any future milestones, however, there is little doubt that the Yankees still want them to be done in pinstripes. Record chasers sell tickets – even if the player is someone who has been as demonized as Alex. So he hit on some women from the dugout during the playoffs. Anyone who has followed the team for the past few decades will brush that off as completely inconsequential. Remember the "Bronx Zoo" Yankees of the 70's? That completely dysfunctional team tore through the majors, winning back-to-back championships in 1977 and 1978. And go back a few years earlier, when two of the Yankees' pitchers, Fritz Peterson and Mike Kekich, swapped wives. They actually swapped entire families – including children and family dogs. Those are headlines. Asking some European model for her phone number is mere child's play.

Then there are the other two numbers.

**14** – With 647 home runs under his belt, Alex is only 14 home runs away from passing Willie Mays for fourth on the all-time Home Runs list. Even with his newly-found lack of power, it is still likely safe to pencil Alex in for at least 20 homers per season, meaning that he will likely pass Mays this year. His next target would be the Babe's 714 (54 ahead of Mays) – and there is little doubt that the Yankee brass does not want to see the Babe dropped another notch by a player whose uniform does not bear the interlocking N-Y.

**99** – Mr. Rodriguez currently has 2,901 career hits. With 99 more hits, therefore, he will attain the magic number 3,000. The last player to reach this milestone was the Yankee captain, Derek Jeter. And Jeter was the first Yankee ever to reach 3,000 hits in pinstripes. What better for Yankee tradition than to have two straight Yankees reach that plateau? And he will likely reach 3,000 this year. It will make great theater – he strokes the hit in Yankee Stadium, and the club's last member, Jeter, saunters out of the dugout to congratulate him? If you think that the Yankee brass would rather see him reach the milestone in another uniform, such as the Marlins' pastel-colored jersey, then you have not been paying attention.

Yesterday, Brian Cashman, Yankee General Manager, said that he expects A-Rod to be the Yankee third baseman next year. While it may be mere lip service, the other fact to consider is that the man rumored to be coming to New York from Miami for Alex, relief pitcher Heath Bell, was actually traded to Oakland last week. Consider that another nail in the coffin of A-Rod trade rumors.

*****

So A-Rod stays – who, then, will not be in the Yankee line-up next year? On this aging and overpaid team, there are several candidates. Let's examine some:

**Russell Martin (catcher)** – Russell did not show a whole lot of muscle last year, certainly not enough to justify his contract. If he wants to stay for $2M, then he can be worth the money. But if he is looking to duplicate last year's $7.5M contract, let him do it elsewhere. Plus, if Austin Romine can come back, he can certainly hit as well as Mr. Martin.

**Rafael Soriano (relief pitcher)** – assuming that Mariano Rivera is coming back, then there is no need for Soriano and his $12M contract. With agent Scott Boras, he will likely be seeking to cash in on his 2012 numbers and pocket even more money. There was no logic to signing him the first time, and clearly no reason to do it again.

**Andruw Jones (outfielder)** – the 63-year old Jones did not leave the bench for what seemed like the last two months of the season – and he hit the ball that led to Rivera's injury. He's done.

**Raul Ibanez (outfielder)** – with three swings of the bat, the 72-year old Ibanez established himself as a Yankee post-season legend. After Game 1 of the Tiger series, however, he regressed and Manager Joe Girardi actually sent the disgraced A-Rod up to pinch hit for him in the last game. If he only wants a minimal contract, like for $2M, then he can contribute. If he is seeking more, however, then he has no place in the Bronx.

**Mariano Rivera (relief pitcher)** – can Mo come back? When the season starts he will be 84 years old. No player of that advanced age has ever come back from such a severe injury. Time will tell.

**Nick Swisher (outfielder)** – the baby on this team of aging superstars, the 14-year old Swisher again disappeared in the playoffs, leading many to call for his expulsion from the team. With a career mark of one hit in 34 post-season at bats with runners in scoring position, even the overly-exuberant man-child cannot justify why the Yankees should continue to pay him in excess of $10M per year.

**Ichiro Suzuki (outfielder)** – the ageless outfielder turned 100 years old during last season, and became the first centenarian to appear in the Major Leagues. Despite concerns about his age, he is a positive force in the dugout and his work ethic should be an influence to players who are one-quarter his age. Also, Ichiro brings in the all-important Asian market to the marketing-savvy Yankees. Lastly, he ranks third among active players with 2,606 hits; with three more good seasons, he can be the third consecutive Yankee (after Jeter and Rodriguez) to reach 3,000. What a publicity coup that will be.

**Hiroki Kuroda (starting pitcher)** - the second half of the Yankees' new "Japanese Dynamic Duo," Kuroda is significantly younger than Ichiro (he is only 58) and has performed well enough to keep his roster spot, especially with questions surrounding the remainder of the starting rotation.

**CC Sabathia (starting pitcher)** – The 458-pound Sabathia is travelling this week to see noted orthopedic surgeon Dr. James Andrews. Nobody goes to visit Dr. Andrews without reason. This does not bode well for the Yankee faithful. He will be back next year but, in light of this surprise doctor visit, when is back may be questionable.

**Phil Hughes (starting pitcher)** – the 26-year old Hughes, who apparently has the back muscles of a 64-year old, is simply too inconsistent. It is time to trade him for someone of value, like a reserve outfielder who can replace Jones and/or Ibanez.

**Eric Chavez (Third baseman)** – handed the third base job when Rodriguez was benched, he responded with a giant o-fer. Tallying no hits in 16 post-season at-bats, with eight strikeouts, is not a way to make a good impression.

**Freddie Garcia and Derek Lowe (pitchers)** – with a combined age of 147, it is time for them to be put out to pasture.

Next year may be a rebuilding year for the Yankees. It is odd when you are rebuilding with a crop of thirty-somethings, but, if the team jettisons some of the *alter cockers,* or old guys, listed above, they will have a chance to again rise to the top of baseball in the future. Just do not expect it during A-Rod's tenure in the Bronx. Not that it matters to him, anyway, as long as he gets his personal numbers up.

Perhaps that is part of the problem.

*writer's note – some of the numbers in the above blog were exaggerated, such as the players' ages or weights. A-Rod's contract amount, however, is real.

**Extra innings:   Many of my predictions came true. The Yankees did intend to keep Rodriguez, until his recovery from hip surgery sidelined him for at least half of the 2013 season and later allegations of PED usage have put his pinstriped career in jeopardy.**

**The Yankees re-signed Hiroki Kuroda to help anchor their pitching staff. They also re-signed Ichiro to start in the outfield, and they are no doubt praying he assaults the 3,000 hit mark with a renewed vengeance. His signing does leave a "power vacuum" in the outfield, however, as neither he nor fellow starter Brett Gardner is known for knocking the ball out of the park.**

**The lack of power will be on full display at season's beginning, as the only power-hitting outfielder, Curtis Granderson, had his right arm broken by an errant pitch in the pre-season and will miss at least the first month of the season, if not more. First baseman Mark Teixeira, whose offensive numbers have steadily declined since his arrival in the Bronx, sustained a wrist injury and will be out until at least May. As Teixeira is an historically slow**

starter (his numbers in April are, career-wise, much lower than the remainder of his statistics), it is therefore fair to assume that he will not truly be a productive member of the offense until mid-June, at the earliest.

In the meantime, the following players (all mentioned above) are no longer members of the team: Russell Martin (signed with Pittsburgh); Rafael Soriano (signed with Washington); Andruw Jones (is going overseas, if the allegations of his domestic violence permit him to do so); Raul Ibanez (signed with Seattle); Nick Swisher (The Ohio native is "going home," having signed with Cleveland); Eric Chavez (signed with Arizona); Derek Lowe (signed a minor league contract with Atlanta); and Freddie Garcia (unsigned).

As far as the others are concerned, it looks like CC Sabathia's visit to Dr. Andrews was a false alarm and he is ready to resume the role of staff ace, whereas Phil Hughes, whom the Yankees inexplicably signed to a $7 million dollar contract for this year, re-injured his elderly back during the pre-season so his status going forward is questionable.

Also, it looks like Austin Romine will either start the year in the minors or as the third-string catcher, behind Chris Stewart and Fernando Cervelli, neither of whom is expected to contribute much offensively. If the Yankees adhere to their new mantra of fiscal prudence and attempt to fill all of their line-up holes internally rather than making any "splashy" free-agent signings or trades, it will be a long year (actually, years) for the Yankee fans.

# SIXTH INNING

## THE METS AND THEIR POOR FANS

I really do not dislike the New York Mets, nor do I hold any contempt for their fans. The Mets are not the Yankees' rivals. They play in different leagues, and even a few games of interleague play cannot create a rivalry which does not truly exist. They do possess, however, what appears to be an extremely dysfunctional organization, from ownership all the way down to the training staff.

What I do dislike is the Mets' fan who actively roots against the Yankees. That simply makes no sense, and is the subject of the second post in this chapter.

The first post in this chapter was actually my initial baseball-related post. I was just having some fun, although it did ruffle some feathers.

# The Plight of the Mets' Fans (July 22, 2009)

In a borough of bruised egos reside the New York Mets
    Almost five decades of playing second fiddle to the Yankees
Unfulfilled promise, drug abuse, and collapses fill their past
    Annually leaving their misguided fans crying in their hankies

Born in 1962, it took only them seven years to climb to the top
    Beating the Orioles in the series they hoped for the future was an omen
But reality has often played its cruel hand of fate
    And they didn't win again till '86 when they squeaked past Boston

And now over two decades later they face
    Annual finishes in fourth, or maybe even fifth place
But oh those teams of the 1980's,
    Anointed as the team of the decade with naturals Darryl and Doc
They only got to the Series that one time in '86
    Resulting in disappointment and anger again for their flock

The bastard child of the Dodgers and Giants
    The orange and blue N-Y a combination of the two
They're always left feeling inferior to the Yankees
    And yearly the fans' discontent grew and grew

Because the Yanks play in the cathedral up in the Bronx
    They have the ghosts, bleacher creatures and YMCA
While up until last year the Mets played in an Orange and blue cupcake
    Named after who else? Why, their attorney William Shea

Now they play in Citifield, in the shadow of the old park
    They look at the new Yankee Stadium and say its size is a sin

But the Mets' new field has no history, and even

      Their vast rotunda is named for a man who didn't play for them

Just look on the wall at their retired numbers, few that they are

      The Franchise, Tom Terrific, number 41, was their only true star

I mean, the others are managers, Hodges and Casey

      Oh, and their owner, the kind and matronly Joan Payson


But it is an unfair comparison for they can't measure up, those poor Mets

      The Yankees have decades of history, 26 titles did they get

Even comparing their best players, the Yanks are far ahead

      Let's do a roll call of the best, whether living or dead


In the outfield the difference is night and day

      The Bronx Bombers have the Babe, Joe D and Mickey

And who, pray tell, can the Mets counter with?

      My best guess is McReynolds, the Stork and Mookie

Go to the infield, not much better for the boys from Queens

      Yanks sport Nettles, Jeter, Lazzari and Gehrig from third to first

And as for the Mets, who will man their star infield?

      Cocaine Keith, Millan, Bud and Babbling Brooks, could do worse

Even looking at catcher, where the Mets have two of their all-time best

      Surely Mike Piazza and Kid Carter could rate

But sadly even at backstop they trail behind the Yankees, who have

      Berra and Dickey, those two fabulous numbers eight


The pitching staff, don't make me laugh

      Once you get past Gooden and Seaver, there's Craig Swan

The Yankees can trot out Louisiana Lightning and Whitey Ford

      Mel Stottlemyre, Andy Pettitte, Boomer Wells and Tommy John

47 years later, what of Mets' no-hitters? That number stands at zero today

      Ryan, Seaver, Gooden, Cone? They all threw theirs after they left Shea

(And remember, Gooden and Cone threw them for the Yankees)


The Hall of Fame, in Cooperstown, just hours from CitiField

    Only one Mets hat is embossed among the plaques on the wall

The Franchise, Tom Terrific, he alone carries the Mets' torch

    The Kid was elected but he proudly wears the Expos' chapeau

And now Piazza is the Mets' only hope to join those in Fame

    But no doubt he'll go in wearing the blue interlocking L-A


It's almost August, time for the Mets' swoon

    This year they'll claim it's because they're all banged up and hurt

But even if they weren't there would be another reason

    'Cause betting on the Mets, you'll always lose your shirt

Just look at Casey, the Old Professor as he was known

    Was a genius with the Yankees but with the Mets he was cursed

The same could be said for Mr. Joe Torre

    Who had the same fortune/misfortune but only in reverse


Many all stars people have gone to Queens just to bust

    George Foster and Eddie Murray in the 80's head the guys

Overpaid and aging all-stars aplenty, much like in the Bronx

    Shea was a place for old ballplayers to have their careers die

See, the Mets play in a division, the National League East

    Fake rivals with the Marlins, Phillies, and Braves

And those pesky Marlins have won as many championships as the Mets

    But did so within one short decade


Yes, 1969 and 1986 are the only times the Mets have won

    So they're usually the bridesmaid, only two times the Bride

It's almost again time to break out your excuses, Mets fans

    And wear them on your blue and orange sleeves with pride

So remember the words of the late Tug McGraw

Mets' fans, "Ya Gotta Believe", but just not this year

Look at it this way, if it makes you feel better

You'll have more time with your family as the playoffs draw near.

**Extra innings:** Events that have transpired since this was written, which would force a re-write so that the poem would be factually correct – the Yankees won the 2009 World Series, so their total is now 27 titles, not 26. Johan Santana pitched the first no-hitter in Mets' history and the Mets have retired Gary Carter's number 8 so they now have two players with retired numbers. Mike Piazza was denied entry into the Hall of Fame in 2013, as detailed in a prior chapter.

**Many players are partially identified above. Their full names are as follows:**

**For the Mets: Darryl (Strawberry), Doc (Dwight Gooden), The Franchise, Tom Terrific (Tom Seaver), (Gil) Hodges, Casey (Stengel) (aka The Old Professor), (Kevin) McReynolds, the Stork (George Theodore), Mookie (Wilson), Cocaine Keith (Hernandez), (Felix) Millan, Bud (Harrelson), (Hubie) Babbling Brooks, (Gary) Kid Carter, (Nolan) Ryan, (David) Cone**

**For the Yankees: Babe (Ruth), Joe D (DiMaggio), Mickey (Mantle), (Graig) Nettles, (Derek) Jeter, (Tony) Lazzari, (Lou) Gehrig, (Yogi) Berra, (Bill) Dickey, (David) Boomer Wells**

As explained in the poem itself, two of the men managed both teams – Casey Stengel and Joe Torre. There was also a third – Yogi Berra. Three of the named players also spent time with each team – David Cone, Dwight Gooden, and Darryl Strawberry.

133

# Hey Met Fan - The Choice is Simple! (October 27, 2009)

The World Series begins tomorrow. It pits the current champions against the seemingly-perennial contenders. It features the past two American League Cy Young award winners, both recent graduates of Cleveland Indian Tech, who will potentially square off three times should the series extend to its full seven games. It will likely serve to further divide the loyalties of the Garden State into its Northern and Southern halves. And, with both teams based in the Northeast, it will no doubt be played in conditions more favorable to football teams battling it out on the gridiron.

Perhaps most importantly, it also serves as a sociological experiment into the mind of that most elusive and misunderstood creature, the Mets' fan. It would seem to most that rooting for the Yankees to win would be an easy decision for the New York faithful, but, based on the tenor on the streets and as being reported in the media, it appears that this is not the case. For many Mets' fans have pledged their allegiance to the Phillies in this series, an unholy matrimony that completely defies the definition of "fandom".

So we pose the question – for whom should the Mets' fans be rooting? Maybe they don't want to see the hometown Yankees win because that will further tip the New York supremacy meter to the pinstriped crowd from the Bronx. But rooting for the Phillies? Incomprehensible, for the men in red are the sworn enemies of the Mets.

Let's examine it a little further. From the beginning of Spring Training, the Mets and Phillies start their annual trash-talking; and that loud-mouthed Jimmy Rollins should be public enemy number one for any Mets fan. The two teams face each other almost twenty times each season, and every win for the Phillies only serves to push the Mets closer and closer to the brink of their eventual elimination. The Phillies have supplanted the Braves as the kings of the

National League Eastern Division, a place where the Mets once held court not so long ago.

In sharp contrast, the Yankees do no trash-talking, or any talking at all, about the Mets. You would have to search long and hard to find a derogatory statement about the Mets attributable to Derek Jeter. In fact, since a steroid-fueled rocket launched a broken bat handle at Mike Piazza in the 2000 Subway Series, one would venture a guess that the Yankees have not even given the Mets a second thought. They play in different leagues, and save six gimmick games a year for interleague play, their paths do not cross except in the local sports pages.

Flash back 23 years. When the Mets played the Red Sox in the 1986 series, all Yankee fans rooted for the denizens of Shea Stadium to crush the crimson-hosed team from New England. Not just because they were from New York. It was because Yankee fans root for the Yankees and anyone who is playing the Red Sox. No questions asked. The same should be true for Mets' fans, they should root for the Mets and whoever is playing the Phillies. It is as simple as that.

Why, then, would a Mets' fan even entertain thoughts of rooting for the Phillies? The answer can only lie in the inferiority complex that lurks within the psyche of the Mets' fan, similar to the jealousy that one might feel for their older, more successful brother. And rather than embracing their kin, they rebel and seek to have misery befall the more successful one, if for no other reason than to make them feel better about themselves. How else can one explain the hatred that the Mets' fans have for the Yankees, other than the fact that it is deeply-rooted in their jealousy? Because the Yankees' fans do not hate the Mets; quite to the contrary, the Mets are not even a blip on the Yankee fans' radar since they are already quite occupied with worrying about Red Sox, Angels and the like.

So for the Blue and Orange–clad fans who are suddenly embracing their enemies from the City of Brotherly Love, it is clear that they are doing so out of spite and jealousy, and are willing to turn their backs on their true allegiance to the Mets in order to fuel their unnecessary hatred of the Bronx Bombers. A true fan of the Mets would root for the team playing their arch-nemesis, the Phillies, even if that team was the Yankees. Or maybe we should say that they would just root harder against the Phillies, but that is just a matter of semantics. It's the same effect. And that way, they would be rooting for the eventual winners.

Yankees in 6.

**Extra innings:   My prediction was correct. The Yankees captured the Series in six games.**

## Why Cliff Lee Should Pack His Bags for NY - to the Mets (?!) (November 6, 2010)

At midnight tonight, the spending spree known as baseball's free agency period commences. It is an annual rite of fall, when all major league teams re-assess their current rosters, consider their financial conditions, and determine if any of the available players on this year's meat market will be the difference between being a contender and making the playoffs or spending another October home with the family.

The undisputed "king of the hill" of this year's free agent pitchers is, of course, Cliff Lee. Despite his World Series missteps over the last couple of weeks, Lee's bravura performances over the past several seasons for a multitude of teams, including his previous post-season successes, will translate into a contract worth well over a hundred million dollars before year's end, if not by Thanksgiving.

Conventional wisdom tells us that only two teams will be seriously wooing Mr. Lee: his current Texas Rangers and the always-free spending New York Yankees -- the back story here is that Lee was shipped to Texas from Seattle earlier this year. Reports had him going to the Yankees for a package of players, and, according to sources, Lee was ecstatic at the time of the prospect of pitching in the Bronx. Somehow, that possibility ended rather quickly, however, and Lee ended up a Ranger, leading his squad to the World Series. During the playoffs against the Yankees, his wife had some type of allegedly negative experience with the New York fans, leading to her mouthing off to the press in what seemed like little more than a pre-emptive justification for Cliff staying in Texas should he decide to do so.

Conventional wisdom, however, is not always correct. And in this instance, the pundits are missing the best landing spot for Mr. Lee and his golden arm, the place which will most benefit him and baseball in general.

137

### The New York Mets.

Wayne Gretzky was traded to the Los Angeles Kings following his record-setting run in Edmonton, in order to spur interest and show that a hockey team could flourish in a warm-weather city. That trade was made not for the benefit of the team, but rather for the good of the entire league – the fact that his wife wanted to increase her acting roles and being closer to tinseltown was an added benefit, but enhancing the league was the driving force behind the deal. Here, baseball's best interest is served by placing its marquee free agent into its biggest market, and having Lee don the blue and orange.

Think about it. The putative kings of Queens are in the midst of a major overhaul. Gone are their ineffective manager and bumbling General Manager. They have brought in baseball-genius Sandy Alderson to run their operations, and he has already begun to assemble a staff that includes some of the best minds in baseball. Rumors have the fiery and beloved Bobby Valentine leaving the comfort of the ESPN studios to return to the Mets' dugout as manager; and if he doesn't get the job, there's another former Mets' manager named Joe Torre who has already expressed an interest in the job. Without even adding a new player, therefore, the Metropolitans are already generating more excitement than they did in their lost 2010 season.

They also have a core of young players who, under proper managing, should flourish this year; including the two faces of the franchise, shortstop Jose Reyes and third baseman David Wright, as well as power-hitting first baseman Ike Davis and outfielders Carlos Beltran and Angel Pagan. The bullpen is still officially anchored by hot-headed Frankie Rodriguez, who, despite leading the league last year in punching girlfriend's fathers, can still be an effective closer. He just took the term "punching them out" a little too literally last year; but maybe a little anger management course will do the trick for him.

Lee can be the anchor of the Mets' pitching staff. The Yankees may have his good friend and former teammate, CC Sabathia, but Lee can step in as the clear ace of the Mets. He can carry the team on his shoulders until mid-summer, when Johan Santana, himself a pretty decent hurler, returns from the disabled list to act as Ace 1-A. If Mike Pelfrey can last an entire season, that will give the Mets a fairly formidable front three, which would serve the team well come the postseason.

Money should be no object for the Mets. They will finally shed Oliver Perez's multi-million dollar fiasco of a contract, and getting rid of money albatross Luis Castillo will also free up significant scratch to throw Lee's way. And there are no other desirable pitching free agents with which the Mets can improve their deficient starting staff – by way of example, one report had 70's-porno mustache-wearing Carl Pavano as the next best hurler on the market, but, remember, he has already proven to be allergic to New York during his ill-fated stint with the Yankees.

It's a new era for the Mets, and if they intend to contend with the Phillies and Braves in their division and, more importantly, if they intend to contend with the cross-town Yankees for space on the New York sports pages, this is the time to open up their wallet. The Mets' owners, the Wilpons, insist that they did not lose millions of dollars to Bernie Madoff's ponzi scheme. Now is the time for them to prove that they are still solvent and committed to bringing a winner to Queens.

The addition of Cliff Lee would give the new-look Mets instant credibility, and would go a great distance toward immediately reversing the mood of doom that has infected Citifield since its opening a couple of years ago. Simply put, having Lee pitch for the Mets will make them a contender, which is good for the Mets and for New York. He will be pitching under less of a microscope than with the Yankees, and if the team wins, he will be regarded as the difference (unlike if he were a Yankee, where he would only be one piece in a puzzle of stars), so pitching for the Mets is good for Lee. And if he can create a winning atmosphere in Citifield, bringing success to the "other team" in the country's biggest media market, then having Lee pitch for the Mets is also good for baseball in general.

*****

Of course, it won't happen. More than likely, Lee will be donning Yankee pinstripes in 2011, and baseball fans across the country will begin screaming anew about how the Yankees are again buying themselves a pennant. And the loudest cries will come from the Mets' fans, frustrated by the fact that their beloved team will be playing second fiddle to the Yankees for yet another season. But this time, they will have their own ownership to blame. Cliff Lee is out there. The Mets can grab him. But they probably won't even make an effort. And that's a shame, if you're a Mets' fan.

**Extra innings: In what was a surprise to many, Lee eventually signed with the Mets' true rivals, the Phillies (see chapter 8). He won 17 games for Philadelphia in 2011, pitching six complete games and recording six shutouts, but slipped to a 6-9 record in 2012, with no complete games and no shutouts.**

**It was later revealed that the Wilpon family and their related entities actually profited greatly from the Madoff ponzi scheme, with reports indicating profits of up to $300 million, leading to a situation where they were the target of a lawsuit by the United States Trustees' Office to disgorge themselves of the monies. They eventually settled with the Trustee's office, reportedly paying over $160 million.**

Interestingly, it was also reported that this was the Wilpons' second go-round with a Ponzi scheme; Madoff, however, claimed that they were completely unaware of his improper activities.

In order to continue operations, the Wilpon family announced that they would sell 49% of the team for $200 million. The buyer, however, was to have no say whatsoever in the running of the team. A deal was allegedly struck at one point, but that buyer soon backed out. The team did receive substantial loans from both Major League Baseball and Bank of America and their front office operations were, for a time, being monitored by Major League Baseball.

# SEVENTH INNING STRETCH

## ALL STAR TEAMS – PLAYERS AND NUMBERS

One of the most time-honored traditions in sports is the comparison of one player to another, of one team to another, and of one era to another. The next five entries deal with such comparisons. The first two deal with determining the best players to wear certain uniform numbers, and the next three focus on creating alphabetical All-Star teams, which is not as easy as it sounds.

# Athletes' Numbers - Who Were the Best Ever? (April 12, 2010)

On April 15, all major league baseball players will wear number 42 to honor Jackie Robinson. It is an annual homage to the man who bravely broke baseball's color line over 60 years ago. And once the Yankees' Mariano Rivera retires, no major leaguer will again wear his number 42, which has been retired by major league baseball. The number, therefore, will always be synonymous with Jackie.

There are other numbers that are so inextricably linked to one player. Number 99 is Wayne Gretzky, so much so that this number has been retired by the NHL. Other iconic numbers include Babe Ruth's #3, Lawrence Taylor's #56, and Mario Lemieux's #66. Michael Jordan's #23 was on that list until recently, but basketball's new king, Lebron James, also wears that number proudly across his Cavaliers' jersey. Then there is the reverse, a number so prevalent that it is a struggle to narrow down a list, like the number 12 worn by, seemingly, every star NFL quarterback in the 70's and 80's.

The mission was to make a list of the greatest players ever to wear a specific number. The main consideration was that the person should, ideally, be retired. And, his number should have been retired by his own team. But there are some current players here, those who have already stamped their tickets for their respective sports' halls of fame when they hang up their spikes, sneakers, or skates.

And I limited it to the four major sports. The big loser because of this rule was Pele, the man who still stands as the face of soccer thirty years after his retirement. The same is true for Diego Maradona, Ronaldinho, Lionel Messi, and the litany of other soccer players who wore number 10, the number usually reserved for the team's greatest player.

I allowed myself up to three people per number, and ranked them in my order of importance. You will note the preponderance of baseballers and, of course, New York players. Clearly, favorites emerge no matter what the debate. That's what makes for lively discussion.

Note: My original intention was to go up to 25. The two top contenders for that number, however, would be Barry Bonds and Mark McGwire and there is no need to glorify them here. So the list stops at 24.

1. *Oscar Robertson, Eddie Giacomin, Ozzie Smith*

2. *Derek Jeter, Moses Malone*

3. *Babe Ruth, Harmon Killebrew*

4. *Lou Gehrig, Bret Favre, Bobby Orr*

5. *Joe DiMaggio, Hank Greenberg, Brooks Robinson*

6. *Stan Musial, Julius Erving, Bill Russell*

7. *Mickey Mantle, John Elway, Pete Maravich*

8. *Yogi Berra, Cal Ripken Jr., Joe Morgan*

9. *Gordie Howe, Ted Williams, Bobby Hull*

10. *Guy LaFleur, Fran Tarkenton, Walt Frazier*

11. *Mark Messier, Isaiah Thomas, Elvin Hayes*

12. *Joe Namath, Terry Bradshaw, Jim Kelly*

13. *Wilt Chamberlain, Dan Marino, Don Maynard*

14. *Bob Cousy, Ernie Banks, Dan Fouts*

15. *Bart Starr, Thurman Munson, Earl Monroe*

16. *Joe Montana, Bob Lanier, Whitey Ford*

17. *John Havlicek, Dizzy Dean*

18. *Peyton Manning, Dave Cowens*

19. *Johnny Unitas, Bob Feller, Robin Yount*

20. *Mike Schmidt, Frank Robinson, Lou Brock*

21. *Roberto Clemente, Warren Spahn, Dominique Wilkins*

22. *Mike Bossy, Emmitt Smith, Jim Palmer*

**23**. *Michael Jordan, LeBron James, Ryne Sandberg*

**24**. *Willie Mays, Kobe Bryant, Bill Bradley*

**Extra innings:** I waffled when I initially posted this one, admitting from the outset that: "The hardest one was number 5 - Albert Pujols, Johnny Bench and George Brett are a pretty formidable threesome." One of the people who commented spewed venom at me for choosing Greenberg over Pujols, but I would not yield. The fact that I considered off-the-field issues, such as his being the first Jewish superstar (see the first chapter) offended the man greatly.

Others were kinder, offering their suggestions without being completely insulting. It was suggested that Tom Brady should have earned a spot over Jim Kelly, which, in hindsight, would probably have made sense. Another suggested that I use Roger Staubach over Kelly or Joe Namath, but I do not think that I would make that switch.

It was also suggested that Gil Hodges should have made the list at #14, although I do not know which of the other three people could be moved to enable his inclusion. Pete Rose was also suggested at #14, although I kept him off of the list for the same reason that I did not consider Barry Bonds or Mark McGwire.

Other suggestions included Carl Yastrzemski at #8, Bobby Clarke at #16 instead of Bob Lanier; Tony Gwynn at #19 over Robin Yount, Barry Sanders at #20 over Lou Brock; and Rickey Henderson at #24 over Bill Bradley. Were I to do it again, I would likely agree with Gwynn, Sanders, and Henderson. Yaz would not surmount any of the other three baseball players at #8, however, and Bobby Clarke would not overtake Lanier.

Last December, in honor of the date 12/12/12, *Sports Illustrated* did a feature on the dozen greatest athletes to wear number 12 – most were quarterbacks (all of the above and Ken Stabler, possibly the second-greatest left-handed QB ever, after Steve Young), and they were joined by several others, including all-time NBA great John Stockton. They also did a 13 best 13 – the first two were the same as above, Wilt Chamberlain and Dan Marino, and then Alex Rodriguez, who appears in almost every other post in this book. Don Maynard was number eight on their list.

# Athletes' Numbers - Who Were the Best Ever? (26-50) (May 29, 2010)

*This was a follow-up to the previous post, with the concept being to pick the best all-time athletes, from the four major sports, who wore numbers 26 through 50.*

I did change the rules a slight bit. Now, for certain of the most popular numbers, I have listed up to four people. Also, several numbers have no entries or only one entry, because the "quality" of players here is, overall, lesser than the first list, or the numbers are not as popular as the lower numbers.

26. *Wade Boggs, Rod Woodson, Billy Williams*

27. *Juan Marichal, Carlton Fisk, Jim "Catfish" Hunter*

28. *Marshall Faulk, Bert Blyleven, Curtis Martin*

29. *Rod Carew, Eric Dickerson, Ken Dryden*

30. *Nolan Ryan, Martin Brodeur*

31. *Dave Winfield, Greg Maddux, Mike Piazza, Reggie Miller*

32. *Sandy Koufax, Jim Brown, Magic Johnson, Steve Carlton*

33. *Kareem Abdul-Jabbar, Larry Bird, Tony Dorsett, Patrick Roy*

34. *Walter Payton, Earl Campbell, Charles Barkley*

35. *Frank Thomas, Phil Niekro, Tony Esposito*

36. *Robin Roberts, Gaylord Perry, Jerome Bettis*

37. *Casey Stengel, Rodney Harrison (both submitted by others)*

38. *Curt Schilling*

39. *Roy Campanella, Larry Csonka, Dominik Hasek*

40. *Gale Sayers*

41. *Tom Seaver, Randy Johnson, Wes Unseld*

42. *Jackie Robinson, Mariano Rivera, Ronnie Lott*

43. *Dennis Eckersley*

44. *Hank Aaron, Willie McCovey, Reggie Jackson, Jerry West*

45. *Bob Gibson*

46. *Andy Pettitte*

47. *Tom Glavine, Jack Morris*

48. vacant

49. *Ron Guidry*

50. *Mike Singletary, David Robinson*

**Extra innings:** Realistically, the numbers 32 and 34 alone could probably fill as many slots as half of the other numbers on this page, several of which have only one entry or, in the case of #48, nobody who made the grade.

Other famous 32's include Karl Malone, Marcus Allen, Elston Howard, Franco Harris, Julius Erving (who appears as #6 in the prior post), Bill Walton and Kevin McHale. One of the best players to wear number 32 was not included because he is now serving time in prison for false imprisonment, after having been incorrectly acquitted of murdering his ex-wife.

Shaquille O'Neal, interestingly, wore both 32 and 34. Hakeem Olajuwon, Rollie Fingers, and Kirby Puckett also wore 34.

# The Best Baseball Team Ever - A to Z (June 9, 2010)

*This post was an attempt to create the best A-Z baseball team. The team would have 24 players, but you had to use different letters for the first letter of the last name of each player. The basic parameters were as follows:*

1. Each letter can only be used once, so two letters would have to be excluded. One is easy, since there has never been a major leaguer whose last name begins with "x".
2. The team should be created "rotisserie baseball" style – two catchers, one 1B, one 3B, one 1B/3B, one 2B, one SS, one 2B/SS, five OFs, one OF/DH, and ten pitchers.
3. Only players who played after World War II are eligible – at least part of their careers. If they never stepped on a baseball diamond after 1945, then they can't play here.
4. They have to be placed in a position where they played the majority of their careers.

And here is my team:

C. *Yogi Berra/Johnny Bench* (tie)

C. *Carlton Fisk*

1B. *Albert Pujols*

3B. *Graig Nettles*

1B/3B. *Gil Hodges*

2B. *Dan Uggla*

SS. *Robin Yount*

2B/SS. *Barry Larkin*

OF. *Hank Aaron*

OF. *Willie Mays*

OF. *Joe DiMaggio*

OF. *Ted Williams*

OF. *Mel Ott*

OF/DH. *Ichiro Suzuki*

SP. *Sandy Koufax*

SP. *Nolan Ryan*

SP. *Bob Gibson*

SP. *Steve Carlton*

SP. *Tom Seaver*

SP. *Randy Johnson*

SP. *Luis Tiant*

SP. *Carlos Zambrano*

RP. *Dennis Eckersley*

RP. *Dan Quisenberry*

So, in alphabetical order, the lineup would read as follows: Aaron (OF), Bench/Berra (C), Carlton (SP), DiMaggio (OF), Eckersley (RP), Fisk (C), Gibson (SP), Hodges (1B/3B), Ichiro (OF), Johnson (SP), Koufax (SP), Larkin (2B/SS), Mays (OF), Nettles (3B), Ott (OF), Pujols (1B), Quisenberry (RP), Ryan (SP), Seaver (SP), Tiant (SP), Uggla (2B), Williams (OF), Yount (SS), Zambrano (P)

Extra innings: One reader suggested that Whitey Ford and Ivan Rodriguez should be inserted instead of Nolan Ryan and Carlton Fisk. Despite the Yankee connection, however, I remain convinced that Ryan and Fisk constitute be a better battery. But ... there was a family outcry over my excluding Derek Jeter – in order to include Jeter, I removed Barry Larkin at SS and starting pitcher Randy Johnson, and then replaced them with two Yankees, Jeter and reliever Sparky Lyle.

One additional side note – this exercise arose out of a challenge made by a friend in the mid-1990's. Back then, you could not complete such a team without using OF Richie Zisk and RP Ugie Urbina, so we are thankful for players who have provided us with the chance to use variety, such as Chase Utley, Dan Uggla, and Carlos Zambrano.

## The All-Star Challenge- Can the AL Measure Up? (July 13, 2010)

*Inspired by the prior posting, a friend put forth his National League All-Star team and I was to counter with my American League squad. It should go without saying that the AL team, with its inclusion of so many Yankee legends, was a better team, at least on paper, than its National League counterpart. Following is the team that I created (Hall of Famers are noted with the HOF designation):*

C. *Yogi Berra (HOF)*

C. *Carlton Fisk (HOF)*

1B. *Hank Greenberg (HOF)*

3B. *Graig Nettles*

1B/3B. *Harmon Killebrew* (HOF)

2B. *Rod Carew (HOF)*

SS. *Derek Jeter (certain future HOF)*

2B/SS. *Roberto Alomar (certain future HOF)*

OF. *Mickey Mantle (HOF)*

OF. *Joe DiMaggio (HOF)*

OF. *Ted Williams (HOF)*

OF. *Carl Yastrzemski (HOF)*

OF. *Willie Upshaw*

OF/DH. *Magglio Ordonez*

SP. *Nolan Ryan (HOF)*

SP. *Jim "Catfish" Hunter (HOF)*

SP. *Jim Palmer (HOF)*

SP. *Bret Saberhagen*

*SP. Frank Viola*

SP. *Luis Tiant*

SP. *Barry Zito*

RP. *Sparky Lyle*

RP. *Dennis Eckersley (HOF)*

RP. *Dan Quisenberry*


So, in alphabetical order, the lineup, which includes thirteen hall of famers, would read as follows: Alomar (2B/SS), Berra (C), Carew (2B), DiMaggio (OF), Eckersley (RP), Fisk (C), Greenberg (1B), Hunter (SP), Jeter (SS), Killebrew (1B/3B), Lyle (RP), Mantle (OF), Nettles (3b), Ordonez (OF), Palmer (SP), Quisenberry (RP), Ryan (SP), Saberhagen (SP), Tiant (SP), Upshaw (OF), Viola (SP), Williams (OF), Yastrzemski (OF), Zito (SP)

While I hadn't prepared a starting lineup, I would probably offer one that looked like this:

SS: Derek Jeter

2B: Rod Carew

OF: Joe DiMaggio

1B: Hank Greenberg

OF: Ted Williams

OF: Mickey Mantle

3B: Harmon Killebrew

C: Yogi Berra

SP: Nolan Ryan

There were a couple of roster changes that I contemplated - the easiest would have been to put either Alex Rodriguez or Cal Ripken at shortstop over Jeter, and then substituting Randy Johnson for Nolan Ryan at starting pitcher. I also wanted to include Robin Yount, but opted for Carl Yastrzemski instead in a no-lose choice between members of the 3,000 hit club. I wanted to include Bob Feller as a pitcher, but could not find a suitable replacement for Fisk at catcher, unless I wanted to plug in Pudge Rodriguez and delete Nolan Ryan.

Magglio Ordonez barely eked out a spot over both Tony Oliva and Amos Otis, but his career numbers are superior. And Willie Upshaw, Frank Viola, and Barry Zito? Consider them as making the best of a bad situation. All were more than servicable, but the simple reality is that there were no better candidates for the letters U, V and Z.

**Extra innings: Not surprisingly, this list contains many of the same players as the prior post, especially due to the preponderance of Yankee representatives.**

**Since this was originally posted, Roberto Alomar was, in fact, elected to baseball's Hall of Fame.**

## **All-Time Yankee All-Star Team: What Team Can Compare?**
## **(bonus entry– never before published)**

*Following the creation of the above All-Star teams, and in the height of Yankee-fan confidence, I formulated the below superstar line-up, comprised entirely of former and current Yankees, with the idea that I would post this team and encourage others to pick a team, or group of teams, and create a line-up which could compare. Realizing that the concept seemed to be a little pompous, I never followed through and never posted this prior to its appearance in this book. It follows the same fantasy baseball team structure as set forth above.*

*C Yogi Berra*

*C. Bill Dickey*

*1B. Lou Gehrig*

*3B. Graig Nettles*

*1B/3B. Don Mattingly*

*2B. Robinson Cano*

*SS. Derek Jeter*

*2B/SS. Tony Lazzeri*

*OF. Babe Ruth*

*OF. Mickey Mantle*

*OF. Joe DiMaggio*

*OF. Dave Winfield*

*OF. Bernie Williams*

*OF/DH. Alex Rodriguez*

*P. Ron Guidry*

*P. Whitey Ford*

*P. Allie Reynolds*

*P. Lefty Gomez*

*P. Mike Mussina*

*P. Red Ruffing*

*P. Mariano Rivera*

*P. Rich Gossage*

*P. Sparky Lyle*

Extra innings: A combination of the three National League teams which played in New York would make a pretty formidable opponent, especially if one were also to include players for the Dodgers and Giants for the time that they have been in Los Angeles and San Francisco. That team could be constructed as follows:

C.         Roy Campanella (Dodgers)

C.         Mike Piazza (Dodgers and Mets)

1B.       Willie McCovey (Giants)

3B.       Matt Williams (Giants)

1B/3B.   Gil Hodges (Dodgers)

2B.       Jackie Robinson (Dodgers)

SS.       Jose Reyes (Mets)

2B/SS.   Pee Wee Reese (Dodgers)

OF.       Willie Mays (Giants and Mets)

OF.       Duke Snider (Dodgers)

OF.       Barry Bonds (Giants)

OF.       Mel Ott (Giants)

OF.       Darryl Strawberry (Mets, Dodgers, Giants – and also Yankees!)

SP.       Sandy Koufax (Dodgers)

SP.     Tom Seaver (Mets)

SP.     Juan Marichal (Giants)

SP.     Don Drysdale (Dodgers)

SP.     Don Newcombe (Dodgers)

SP.     Orel Hershiser (Dodgers, Giants)

SP.     Christy Mathewson (Giants)

RP.     John Franco (Mets)

RP.     Brian Wilson (Giants)

This is a pretty good line-up, but still not good enough to beat the Yankees offensively. Then again, the starting pitching staff - especially a top four of Koufax, Seaver, Marichal and Drysdale - is better than that of the Yankees so, if pitching does in fact beat hitting, perhaps the Yankee team would go down in defeat.

Note also that there were numerous other All-Star caliber pitchers left off of this staff, most notably Carl Hubbell (Giants), Fernando Valenzuela (Dodgers), Don Sutton (Dodgers), Gaylord Perry (Giants), and Carl Erskine (Dodgers).

The dream match-up would be 1978 Ron Guidry (25-3 record, 16 complete games, and a microscopic 1.74 ERA) v. 1963-1966 Sandy Koufax (over that four-year period, he averaged a record of 24-7, 22 complete games, 1.85 ERA, and 307 strikeouts). Even with the remarkable group of hitters on the two squads above, the likelihood would exist for a 1-0 final score. On a Babe Ruth home run, perhaps.

# EIGHTH INNING

## OTHER BASEBALL-RELATED BLOGS

These are a collection of what I will term "miscellaneous" posts. Only the first deals with actual on-the-field events, and celebrates a man who is one of only a handful of players to garner the game-winning hit to clinch two World Series titles. The next concerns a man who hit one of the biggest World Series home runs in Yankee history, but focuses not on that hit, but a devastating hit of a different kind.

The final two can best be described as surreal. One deals with a racist ex-ballplayer and his hatred of President Obama, and the second details the failed extortion efforts of a would-be gay lover and his intended target, pitcher Carl Pavano.

## Edgar Renteria - Best Colombian Baseball Player Ever (November 2, 2010)

*"Adios Pelota"* – with the score tied at zero in the seventh inning of last night's World Series Game 5, Edgar Renteria strode to the plate with a chance to win the championship for his team. *Again.* And with one swing of his bat, the Barranquilla, Colombia native blasted a home run into the left field stands, permitting radio announcer Jon Miller to exercise his knowledge of the Spanish language and providing the Giants with a 3-0 lead that they would never relinquish. It proved to be the game-winning hit in San Fran's 3-1 clinching victory. With one swing of the bat, he ended the pitchers' duel that had been waged between the respective staffs' aces, Tim Lincecum and Cliff Lee, and again exposed Lee as, at least in this World Series, being merely mortal.

More importantly, it was the second time that Renteria had the game-winning hit in a World Series-clinching game. In 1997, his 11th inning single lifted the Florida Marlins to their first-ever championship over the Cleveland Indians. And on another occasion, he actually had the reverse fortune, making the last out as a member of the St. Louis Cardinals as the Boston Red Sox swept their way to the 2004 crown, their first championship in 86 years.

Renteria has, therefore, had the game-winning hit for a franchise winning its first-ever World Series (1997 Marlins), made the last out to enable a team to break the most famous curse (of the Bambino, that is) in sports history (2004 Red Sox) and bashed a home run to catapult one of baseball's most storied franchises to its first World Series title in over half a century, and its first since its move to the West coast (2010 Giants). If ever someone could be counted on to make a historic difference in the fortunes of a baseball team, clearly, it is Edgar Renteria.

That is a pretty impressive resume. And no doubt last night's homer caused as many people to dance in the streets of Barranquilla as another

159

celebrity from that Colombian city, singer Shakira. And as if keeping company with the gorgeous pop superstar isn't enough, Renteria is only the fourth player in Major League history to have two World Series-clinching hits. He is also the first player in history to do so while wearing uniforms that did not contain Yankee pinstripes. The other three players were pretty decent players in their own right – Yankee legends Lou Gehrig, Joe DiMaggio, and Yogi Berra. That's some pretty great company.

As far as players hailing from Colombia, however, Renteria stands alone. Especially today, as he basks in the glow of another clutch hit and, for the second time in his career, is able to boast that his hit was the difference, and that his bat carried his team to championship glory. *Adios pelota* indeed.

**Extra innings:   Renteria retired after the 2011 season, having played with seven different teams over a 15-year major league career. He finished with 2,327 career hits, 140 home runs, 923 runs batted in, 294 stolen bases, and a career batting average of .286. He captured the 2010 World Series MVP award following his last-game heroics and was a five-time All-Star. He also won three Silver Slugger awards (best hitter at his position) and two Gold Glove awards.**

**There have only been thirteen major leaguers who hailed from Colombia. The only one with a career span comparable to Renteria's was Orlando Cabrera, who broke into the majors in 1997, one year after Renteria, and who also played his last game in September of 2011. Cabrera was also a shortstop, and played for nine teams – over half of his career with the Montreal Expos and one season or less for several teams. He finished with career totals of 2,055 hits, 123 home runs, 854 runs batted in, 216 stolen bases, and a .272 batting average. He also won the Gold Glove award two times. These are respectable statistics, but not quite as good as Renteria's.**

Cabrera did share, however, Renteria's knack for historic at-bats. In 1999, he made the last out in a perfect game which was pitched by the Yankees' David Cone. He was also a member of the Red Sox team which won the 2004 World Series over Renteria's Cardinals.

# Former World Series Hero is Florida's New Version of O.J. (November 20, 2010)

Jim Leyritz played eleven seasons in the Major Leagues, and was a two-time World Series champion with the New York Yankees. He tallied 667 hits and slugged 90 home runs during his career. In October of 1996, Jim Leyritz smashed a home run which is, to this day, credited with turning the momentum of the World Series and catapulting the Yankees to the championship that year over the Atlanta Braves.

His most resounding hit, however, took place seven years after he last stepped onto the baseball diamond as an active player. In December 2007, Jim Leyritz, long since retired from baseball, ran a red light and crashed his truck into another vehicle, killing a mother of two.

Today, a Florida jury found him innocent of DUI manslaughter, convicting him only of a misdemeanor DUI offense.

Obviously, we cannot convict someone based solely on what we have read in the newspapers over the almost three years since the fatal crash. As an attorney whose practice includes the defense of people accused of offenses and crimes, including DUI offenses, I should not, in any way, question the verdict handed down by the Florida jury.

I shouldn't, but I will. The testimony offered by the Prosecutor's office indicated that Leyritz's blood alcohol content [BAC] was 0.14, a level which is almost double the Sunshine State's 0.08 legal limit for DUI. Other evidence offered by the Prosecution is that the former World Series hero, who was out that evening celebrating his birthday, had consumed approximately a dozen shots of liquor before leaving the bar and colliding with his victim's vehicle at approximately 3:00 that morning.

The defense team offered clever excuses, including the possibility that a concussion sustained by the former catcher in the accident may have slowed down the alcohol absorption in his body. They also argued that his BAC was possibly less than the 0.08 legal limit at the time of the crash, and that it was possible that he had entered the intersection under a yellow light, rather than red.

No doubt the defense did not tell the jurors of the fact that Leyritz had already paid the victim's family $350,000 in order to settle a wrongful death civil lawsuit that they had previously brought against him.

Earlier this week, another iconic former New York athlete, Dave Meggett, was sentenced to 30 years in prison for sexual misconduct. Two other former New York Giants (Mark Ingram and Plaxico Burress) are in the middle of prison terms for their own transgressions, and it will not be long before Lawrence Taylor's fate is decided when his own rape trial goes before a New York jury. It was widely expected that when Leyritz's trial concluded, he would be joining the ex-New York chain gang.

Instead, it appears that a razzle-dazzle defense team and, possibly, the allure of being an ex-athlete, have again allowed a person to escape conviction on the serious charges facing them. It brings to mind, of course, a certain retired football legend who was incredibly acquitted of murder charges over a decade ago in California. And like that miscarriage of justice, this does not appear to be a verdict to be celebrated, even by those who previously toasted Leyritz's accomplishments on the baseball diamond.

Today, in state known for the juice of a certain citrus fruit, it is evident that Jim Leyritz has taken his place as Florida's O.J.

**Extra innings: One other factor in the Leyritz decision may have been that the other driver, the woman killed in the crash, allegedly had a BAC of**

0.18, even higher than Leyritz's. In reality, however, that the other driver was also drunk could not properly absolve Leyritz of liability.

Leyritz served as pitching coach for the minor league Newark Bears in 2011, and in 2012, he returned to the Yankee family, under an unspecified "personal services contract".

Plaxico Burress returned to the NFL after his release from prison, having served time after pleading guilty to a felony weapon possession charge – arising out of his having shot himself in the leg while in a New York City nightclub. Since his return, has played for both the Jets and his original team, the Steelers. He has not had any additional gun-related incidents.

Mark Ingram was sentenced to seven years in prison for money laundering and fraud in 2008. He failed to turn himself in to begin serving his sentence and was captured in a hotel room pursuant to an arrest warrant while trying to watch his son, Mark Ingram, Jr., a running back for the University of Alabama, play in the 2009 Sugar Bowl. He was incarcerated and could not attend the ceremony when his son won the 2009 Heisman Trophy as outstanding college football player.

Lawrence Taylor later pleaded guilty to patronizing a prostitute and to having sex with a minor. He was placed on probation for six years. The underage prostitute with whom he had sex later brought a civil suit against him, but the jury, after deliberating for only 50 minutes, ruled in Taylor's favor.

## Cliff Lee to the Phillies?? Merry Christmas, Philadelphia (December 14, 2010)

Cliff Lee signed with the Phillies last night. Reports have him accepting a five-year offer to return to the City of Brotherly Love after a one-year hiatus, thereby ensuring that the land of cheesesteaks will enjoy a very happy Christmas "Halladay" season. In so doing, he also broke the hearts and spirits of last year's American League Championship Series contenders, leaving both the Yankees and Rangers without the ace starter that they each so coveted.

Lee was the best pitcher on the free agent market, a virtual Secretariat to the rest of the available hurlers – to show the dearth of available pitching, Carl Pavano (cough) is recognized as the second-best. And by inking him for the next half-decade, the Phillies have provided their fans with the best starting foursome that the major leagues have seen in decades - Roy Halladay, Cliff Lee, Roy Oswalt, and Cole Hamels. The only rotation in recent memory that can even come close, possibly, would be the Atlanta Braves' starters of the '90s, a staff that included Greg Maddux, Tom Glavine, John Smoltz, and a pre-injury Steve Avery. It is certainly far better than the Yankees' current rotation, which, if Andy Pettitte decides to retire, will seemingly consist of CC Sabathia, Phil Hughes, Larry, Moe, and Curly (the *"Three Stooges"*, for anyone confused).

It has been a strange and surprising off-season, to say the least. The Red Sox took their fishing pole and snared the fastest Ray available (*Carl Crawford*), and also enticed a slugging Padre to forego his religious vows in exchange for untold millions of dollars (*Adrian Gonzalez*). The Nationals spent $126 million dollars for an outfielder, far more than anyone else believed he was (*Jayson*) Werth, and the free-spending Yankees have been left holding their satchel of money, with nobody willing to accept their bountiful gifts. And now, Mr. Lee, the most coveted free agent since a King (*Basketball star Lebron James*) fled Cleveland, has landed in Philadelphia, to, it appears, the surprise of everyone. The only thing missing from the whirlwind courtship undertaken by

165

the Yankees' and Rangers' owners was a "decision" show similar to the one that ESPN aired with James' - *"Well, I've decided to take my talents to South Beach, oops, I mean South Philly"*.

The solace to Yankees' fans is that Lee, in all likelihood, was not the answer to their problems. He cannot bring the fountain of youth to the Bronx, and showed in the World Series last year that he is no longer invincible come October. He will likely do better within a rotation where he has more than one other starter beside him, and his signing makes the Phillies the new favorite to capture the Series this coming season.

The likelihood is that it will be the ultimate "patriotic" series, featuring two cities so integral to the formation of the United States over two centuries ago, with the Phillies prevailing over the Boston Red Sox. Independence Hall triumphing over Faniuel Hall. William Penn will be drinking a celebratory beer courtesy of John and Sam Adams. The Liberty Bell will ring (very carefully, of course), as opposed to celebratory lights being illuminated in Old North Church. So the Yankees' fans can rejoice over that *fait accompli*.

There is not much more to say about Lee going to the Phillies, except to congratulate the Phillies' phaithphul phans.

**Extra innings:** **There was no such patriotic theme in the 2011 World Series, as the St. Louis Cardinals triumphed over the Texas Rangers - the Phillies lost to the eventual champion Cardinals in the first playoff round, and the Red Sox did not even make it into the postseason, losing on the season's final day to keep them out of the playoffs. Both the Phillies and Red Sox then stumbled through a middling 2012, and Lee finished the year with a below-average record of six wins and nine losses.**

None of the other 2011 off-season acquisitions noted above proved to be worth the monies spent to get them – the Red Sox have already shed themselves of Crawford and Gonzalez, trading them to the Dodgers, and Werth saw his batting average plummet by over 60 points in his first season as a Washington National. Last year, he saw action in only 81 games due to injuries, and managed to slug only five home runs, far less than the 29 homers that he averaged over his last three seasons in Philadelphia. See pages 106 through 110 for a more detailed discussion of the Red Sox acquisitions and the continued free-spending of certain baseball teams.

## Obama or the Devil for President? One Racist Sounds Off (June 5, 2012)

Imagine a presidential contest between Barack Obama and the Devil. For whom would you cast your vote? To former major league pitcher and perpetual sound bite John Rocker, the choice is simple – Beelzebub all the way. According to WorldNetDaily, Rocker would cast his vote for the Prince of Darkness, quoting Rocker as follows: *"In my strong opinion Barack Obama does not hold a single core value or belief consistent with the principles that created this amazing country we call the United States of America ... I would vote for the devil himself over Barack Obama, which would actually be tough, though, as he seems to already be a supporter."*

These are pretty strong words from Rocker, although we must remember that this is the same man who insulted all of New York years ago while he was employed as a relief pitcher for the Atlanta Braves. During an interview with *Sports Illustrated* in late 1999, which was published in January 2000, Rocker said that he would not want to play for either of New York's teams, because:

*"I'd retire first. It's the most hectic, nerve-racking city. Imagine having to take the 7 Train to the ballpark looking like you're riding through Beirut next to some kid with purple hair, next to some queer with AIDS, right next to some dude who just got out of jail for the fourth time, right next to some 20-year-old mom with four kids. It's depressing... The biggest thing I don't like about New York are the foreigners. You can walk an entire block in Times Square and not hear anybody speaking English. Asians and Koreans and Vietnamese and Indians and Russians and Spanish people and everything up there. How the hell did they get in this country?"*

A pressured Rocker issued a less-than-heartfelt apology at the insistence of Baseball Commissioner Bud Selig, but years later felt the need to lambaste Selig for forcing him to make this apology and (allegedly) attend sensitivity training. I say "allegedly" because reports during his playing career also had him insulting women, gays, and blacks, once allegedly referring to African-American teammate Randall Simon, for example, as a fat monkey.

During his six-year major league career, Rocker amassed a total of 88 saves to go with his countless insensitive remarks. He saved 38 and 24 games during 1999 and 2000, respectively, while pitching for the Braves, and then totaled 23 saves in 2001, splitting his time between the Braves and Indians. The next two years included stops in Texas and Tampa Bay before he left the major leagues for good. Following his retirement, he was named in a steroids probe and, last year, he admitted to the use of performance-enhancing drugs during his career, further staining his reputation.

So perhaps voting for the Devil is not out of character for Rocker. The same report noted that he originally supported Newt Gingrich for President, and has now thrown his support behind presumptive Republican nominee Mitt Romney. Thus far, there has been no comment from the Romney camp, but it is highly doubtful that Rocker's comments will be used by the campaign in any of their upcoming literature.

**Extra innings:  As is well-known, Barack Obama was re-elected president in November 2012 over Republican Mitt Romney. The official tallies made no mention of how many votes were cast for the Devil, so it is impossible to know how well Rocker's candidate fared. The front page of Rocker's website, which contains a mission statement penned in September of 2006, focuses on the "Speak English Campaign" which is devoted to having everyone in the United States speaking English – because in his mind, any immigrants who come to this country and do not make efforts to learn the language and practice American customs are "showing a tremendous lack of respect" for those who sacrificed to make this country "great".**

169

Another entry on the site is simply entitled "True Cost of Illegals ... Disgrace". It does appear, however, that the site has not been updated since the entry of the above mission statement, so perhaps Mr. Rocker will come to realize that he is, thankfully, (with the exception of the buzz created by the Obama v. Devil comment) irrelevant.

## I'll Tell People You're Gay if You Don't Give Me a Car (March 30, 2012)

Extortion, by its very definition, is not a clean business. This week, however, extortion took on new heights (lows?) of ridiculousness when a former classmate attempted to extort a Range Rover from Minnesota Twins pitcher Carl Pavano. The man, Christian Bedard, threatened to expose a homosexual relationship between him and Pavano unless he received an apology, as well as a navy blue Range Rover SUV with tan interior.

The specificity of the vehicle's colors, however, was not even the strangest part of this demand. The truly odd part was that the threat was not even made to Pavano himself. Instead, Bedard issued his extortion demands to Pavano's sister, and he did it through Facebook. Bedard allegedly sent Pavano's sister numerous messages through Facebook, claiming that he was writing a book which would contain allegations of a homosexual relationship between him and Pavano unless Pavano provided him with the above-requested apology and vehicle.

There have been no reports, however, about whether anyone else "liked" the Facebook messages.

Moreover, Bedard apparently claimed that he was to receive a $1.2 million dollar advance to write the book, and that he was willing to give up that advance if he received the "I'm sorry" and his blue-and-tan cruising vessel. This claim is incredible on at least a couple of levels. First, who would give up over a million dollars for one vehicle, which, even if fully loaded, does not cost more than $100,000? It simply does not make economic sense. Also, a little reality check is in order. What publisher would be willing to give an unknown author, with an unsubstantiated story, over a million dollars? Who would give him that much money for a story about Carl Pavano? Carl Pavano? Clearly there was no such advance in the works.

No charges have yet been filed against Bedard. In a statement, Bedard, who is 36 and lives with his mother, claimed that: *"I have been openly gay for most of my adult life ... For years, my physical high school relationship with Carl Pavano has been well-known to my close friends and family. Carl Pavano's sister, Michelle DeGennaro, contacted me on Facebook asking under what conditions would I not talk about my relationship with Carl."* He further stated that the Range Rover request was made in jest.

Pavano's sister disagrees with this account, and reported the threats to police. She also maintains that her brother is not gay. Pavano, citing the advice of counsel, has declined to comment. He has sported a large, Tom Selleck-like 1970's porno mustache for some time now, but, if one recalls the *"Seinfeld"* ménage-a-trois episode, that does not make him gay, it just means that he may be an "orgy person". There have been no other allegations about Pavano being a homosexual, and it appears that this was simply a misguided attempt by an old classmate to cash in on the success of a professional athlete.

Besides, if Pavano owes anyone a Range Rover, it should be given to me, but for an entirely different reason. In December 2004, Pavano, then with the Montreal Expos, signed a four-year contract with the Yankees for the outrageous sum of $39.95 million dollars. Shoulder injuries limited him to only four victories in the 2005 season. In 2006 he suffered a buttocks injury in spring training (in the spirit of good taste, no joke being inserted here) and then later broke two ribs in a car accident. 2007 brought questions about his performance from teammates, and he only started one game (and earned one win) for the Yankees. There was scant little more success in 2008, and Pavano ended his four-year term in the Bronx with a total of nine victories, or a cool $4.44 million dollars per win. He threw a total of 145 major-league innings during that stint, meaning that he was paid $275,517 per inning, or almost $92,000 per out.

Those numbers are simply ridiculous, and Yankees' fans deserve restitution. It should not be difficult to figure out. He was paid almost $40 million dollars. The Yankees averaged about four million fans each of the seasons that he "played," and I use that term loosely, in the Bronx. That means that there were 16 million fans total, and that each is therefore entitled to $2.50 from Pavano. I went to numerous games over that span, however, and am therefore entitled to more; also, like an attorney in a class-action suit, and since I am the "lead plaintiff" in this request, I should be entitled to additional monies. So I want a Range Rover.

And no, Carl, I have no juicy stories to tell about you. Sadly, the reasons that you owe me and so many others money is a matter of public record. Just let me know when you are sending it over. And please, I don't want it in blue with tan leather interior. I will take silver. Thank you.

**Extra innings: I originally wrote this piece as a joke, and was going to continue the theme here by noting that I have not yet received my Range Rover. The topic of gays in professional sports, however, has become a hot-button issue, especially in light of recent comments made by professional baseball and football players both for and against having homosexual players in the locker room. It is important to note that there have been several former players who have come out of the closet following their playing days, including baseball players Glenn Burke and Billy Bean, but no player has ever revealed that he was gay while still actively playing.**

**During last year's NFL playoffs, Chris Culliver of the San Francisco 49ers stated that gays would not be welcome in the locker room, saying that he could not be with "that sweet stuff". His comments drew the ire of many, including Baltimore Ravens linebacker Brendon Ayanbadejo, an outspoken supporter of gay rights. Recently, an NFL prospect was asked by one team's representative whether he "likes" girls. An investigation is now pending as to which team it was and whether sanctions will be levied.**

**When asked whether a player should admit to being gay, Ayanbadejo stated that the player should lie about his sexuality in order to be drafted,**

sign a contract, and make the team. Then, he added, once the player was able to establish himself as a player, and when "we break down some of these walls in the NFL," then the player could come out and be "comfortable to really be who they are." He then compared the first gay player to Jackie Robinson, saying that such a player would be a "pioneer for gay rights and equality."

Even more progressive is Tigers' ace and former Cy Young Award winner Justin Verlander, who was quoted in early March 2013 as saying that a gay baseball player should feel comfortable coming out – "[g]iven the right situation and a team that has a family atmosphere, absolutely. We have that here. I don't think one of our players would be afraid to come out. What your sexual orientation is, I don't see how that affects our goals as a family."

Former Brewers' reliever Mark Knudsen had penned a piece in *Mile High Sports* days earlier, and his beliefs clearly disagree with Verlander's. Knudsen's positions were vehemently anti-gay, as he wrote that anyone pressing an "individual agenda," such as gay rights, would be acting in a manner opposite to a "team" concept. Also, he worried that a gay athlete would no doubt take notice of the other athletes in the locker room, as athletes are "some of the most physically fit and desirable human beings on the planet." In his mind, gays should keep their sexual orientation private while actively playing, so as not to interfere with the team's best interests and to not make any of the other players feel uncomfortable.

While Knudsen's comments are offensive, the unfortunate reality is that athletes do have reason to avoid revealing their sexuality. Despite Verlander's belief that such athletes would be accepted by their teammates, the likelihood is that that there would be more than enough Knudsens and Cullivers to make that athlete's life miserable.

The comparison to Jackie Robinson is to be expected, but is not entirely accurate. Robinson was brought into the league as the first African-American major league player. He showed tremendous courage in doing so, and tremendous restraint in not responding to the catcalls and insults that were hurled at him from city to city. But Robinson could not hide who he was in order to get a better contract or to be accepted by teammates. A gay athlete, in contrast, can hide himself and take steps to convince others that he is heterosexual.

This situation is perhaps more akin to Hank Greenberg's. As discussed in the first post in this book, Greenberg was one of the first openly Jewish ball players. Others before him changed their names to avoid their religion from being exposed. Greenberg showed the courage to keep his name, to wear his religion proudly, and to serve as a role model for Jews across this country.

Judaism, however, is a religion. Homosexuality is not. Even though Anti-Semitism and racism against African-Americans still exist in this country, certainly more than we want or would have hoped would be the case in 2013, the "anti-gay" lobby, including the athletes noted above, is stronger than such bigotry when it refers to athletes and locker rooms. Even as gays gain the right to marry in some states, therefore, it appears that such acceptance in locker rooms is still beyond reach.

A college baseball player, Sean Karson of MIT, recently exhibited a tremendous amount of bravery in coming out to his teammates. He reported that the response was largely positive. The program at MIT, however, is not sports at a professional level nor is it one of college's premier programs, and it would be folly to presume that the reaction of players at that school are at all indicative of how reaction would be at big-time college programs or in the NFL or Major League Baseball.

# NINTH INNING

## THE CLOSER

It is fitting that the final chapter be devoted to the man who has nailed down the final inning of so many games for the Yankees over the past decade and a half, Mariano Rivera. He has already been mentioned in previous posts, but the following two posts focus mainly on him and his astounding performance in the Bronx since his ascension to the role of "closer" for the team. The first compares him, favorably, to all other relievers in baseball history, and the second laments the possible end of his career. Thankfully for Yankees' fans, the second one's basic thesis is incorrect and Rivera is returning to pitch in 2013.

## Mariano Rivera Sets the Saves Mark, But is He the Best Ever? (September 20, 2011)

Yesterday, the Yankees' Mariano Rivera retired three straight Minnesota Twins to notch his 602nd career save and, with that perfect ninth inning, secured the top spot among Major League Baseball's all-time saves leaders. He moved one ahead of Trevor Hoffman, who retired last year after compiling 601 career saves. And even in his 40's, Mariano shows little signs of slowing down. This save was his 43rd of the 2011 season, and there is no reason to believe that he will not reach 650, if not more, before he eventually retires.

Sportswriters and the Yankee faithful, not surprisingly, are hailing "Mo" as the greatest reliever ever to play the game. There is much statistical support for this proposition, of course: in addition to the 602 saves, which have been compiled over a 15-year span, Rivera also possesses the most post-season saves (42, perhaps appropriately as he wears uniform number 42) as well as a microscopic post-season ERA of 0.70. So while he has had the most opportunities to pitch in the post-season by virtue of pitching for perennial playoff-bound New York, he has certainly made the most of these opportunities. He has never had less than 28 saves in a season since becoming the Yankees' closer in the late 1990's, and his durability has been nothing short of remarkable.

But is he the greatest reliever of all time? That certainly is open to debate. He is without question the greatest closer of all-time; that is, he is the best at pitching one inning or less and finishing off games, as the role has come to be defined over the past couple of decades. In an era spawned by Oakland's Dennis Eckersley and others, an era dominated by seventh and eighth-inning specialists and lefty/righty specialists, Mariano stands alone atop the leader board. There can be no doubt.

When one considers all relievers, and opens the discussion up to prior eras, however, then the issue becomes more clouded.

Sports are rife with debates about the best players, especially when one tries to compare one era to another. Deciding the best reliever of all time is no different. And to some, the debate will come down to two pitchers – each of whom pitched for the Yankees and struck fear in the hearts of opposing batters – Mariano Rivera and Rich Gossage. There are no easy answers to this question; it is much like Colts' fans arguing over who was the better quarterback, Johnny Unitas or Peyton Manning. Or Lakers' fans arguing over who was better, Magic Johnson or Kobe Bryant. Each side can make cogent arguments to support their position. The fact that the players were from different eras, with different styles of play and differing requirements in order to master their position, makes the debate all the more difficult.

The 1970's-era relievers were a much different breed than today's closers. Today, the "closer", as the role has been defined, consists mainly of pitchers who never see the mound prior the ninth inning. Even if the game is on the line in the seventh or eighth inning, managers are loathe to bring in their closer for fear that he will then not be able to pitch the ninth inning and "close" the game. The 70's were different. In that decade, and until Oakland's Tony LaRussa began to use Eckersley and the rest of the A's bullpen in more defined (by inning, that is) roles, the term "closer" was not used. Relievers were known as "firemen." They were used to squelch potential rallies by the opposing team, whether those rallies were in the seventh, eighth, or ninth innings. As the afore-mentioned Rich Gossage, a member of the Hall of Fame, has always been quick to point out, he still holds the record for most saves consisting of two or more innings of work.

Those 70's relievers were a scary, surly bunch. Much has been made of the Giants' Brian Wilson and his *"fear the beard"* persona. Now, he seems like a unique individual. Back then, he would have simply fit in with the crowd. "Goose" Gossage had a giant fu Manchu and his hulking figure made him look like a giant on the mound. Bruce Sutter, one of the other greats from that era, sported a beard that rivaled Wilson's while pitching for the Cubs, Cardinals, and

Braves. The Yankees' Sparky Lyle sported a giant, bushy mustache, and Rollie Fingers brought the handlebar mustache back into style for Oakland and Milwaukee.

And then there was Al Hrabosky, perhaps the wildest of them all. Nicknamed "The Mad Hungarian", Hrabosky also sported a thick fu Manchu – and he would whip the Kansas City (and, later, Atlanta and St. Louis) crowd into a frenzy when he would step off behind the mound, rub the ball furiously, and then slam the ball into his glove while wheeling around and returning to the pitching rubber to face a batter. It was a theatrical show that would not be tolerated in today's game. It was intimidating. He was, if nothing else, the precursor to Mr. Wilson and his beard.

Gossage, Sutter, and Eckersley are all enshrined in the Hall of Fame. As such, the debate over who was the best, if not Mariano, must begin and end with them. A case could be made for Eckersley, who redefined the role of closer after a successful career as a starting pitcher – he retired with over 200 victories and 300 saves, remarkable numbers by any standard. Sutter was the dominant reliever in the National League over his career, even when pitching for lousy teams in the 70's. Lee Smith, not yet enshrined in Cooperstown, was the saves record holder prior to Hoffman, which apparently seems to many, including the Hall of Fame voters, more a testament to his longevity, so he does not merit consideration here.

Which leaves Gossage, who, as noted above, still holds the record for two-inning or more saves. At a time when pitchers would routinely go two innings or more in order to garner a save, the "Goose" was the most intimidating. Now, in an era where pitchers rarely see more than one inning of work in order to get a save, Rivera is, with his cut fastball, the most intimidating. So is either "better" than the other? Perhaps not. Each man dominated the position. Each set a standard by which others can be measured.

One is in the Hall of Fame. The other is a lock to be enshrined in his first year of eligibility.

In the end, more people will consider Rivera the best ever due to his number of saves. Assuming he retires in the 650 range, a pitcher would have to average more than 40 saves per year over a 16-year period just to equal that mark. A glance at today's rosters does not reveal any pitchers who will likely endure for that long, much less with that level of greatness. And I would tend to agree. Although we usually romanticize the past, which would enable me to remember days sitting on the couch and watching the fearsome Goose mow down batter after batter for the 1978 champions, I have been equally privileged to watch Mariano Rivera for the past 15 years, to listen to the strains of *"Enter Sandman"* as he jogged to the mound, and watch him raise his hand time and again after nailing down victory after victory, both in the regular season and playoffs/ World Series. This vote is for Rivera.

**Extra Innings: As set forth in the next post, Rivera suffered a devastating knee injury last May and missed most of the 2012 season. His record currently sits at 608 regular season saves – but he is returning for the 2013 season (his final year) and will undoubtedly add to that total.**

As noted above in Chapter Two, Gossage continues to be one of the more vocal ex-ballplayers, calling for the exclusion of any accused PED users from the Hall of Fame. Gossage, who makes no secret of his derision of current players as opposed to himself and other former players, also continues to state that the relievers of today have it easier than when he pitched. When Rivera announced his retirement on March 9, 2013, Gossage praised him, but then self-servingly added: *"The last thing I want to do is take anything away from this guy, he is great. But I would throw out the challenge that, do what we did and we'll compare apples to apples. We didn't get to pitch just one inning."*

# Mariano Rivera Tears ACL ... Hall of Fame Career Likely Over (May 4, 2012)

*... and why I hate Yankees' outfielder Andruw Jones.*

Yesterday, seemingly, the Hall of Fame career of Yankee closer Mariano Rivera came to a crashing halt. Shagging flies in Kansas City before that evening's game between the Yankees and Royals, as he had done so often over his 18-year career, Rivera sustained severe damage to his right knee, tearing his right ACL and sustaining damage to his meniscus. At age 42, the likelihood of a recovery which would enable him to keep playing is slight. More than likely, we have seen the last of Rivera's reign as the Yankees' premier reliever.

More appropriately, we have seen the last of Rivera's reign as baseball's premier reliever. Assuming that he does not return to the baseball diamond, Rivera will retire with an all-time record 608 career saves. No other active player has more than 370. The only way that this saves record will be broken is if the number two man on the list, Trevor Hoffman, somehow convinces a team to sign him up so that he can try for eight additional saves and regain the record that he held before it was broken by Rivera last year. Note that the 608 number can be inflated even higher if you count Mo's post-season statistics (42 saves), which also were record-shattering.

Last September, Rivera notched save number 602, passing Hoffman and solidifying the positions of those who opined that he was the greatest reliever ever. There is no reason to change that opinion now. And, most assuredly, there will be no reason to change that opinion during the course of our lifetimes. Mariano Rivera was part of the "core four", the backbone of the New York team that won five World Series championships since 1996. There was no reliever in the game who was more reliable – and his loss leaves a tremendous void at the back end of the Yankees' bullpen.

His loss also means the official "retirement" of the number 42 – the number was retired by Major League Baseball some years ago to honor Jackie Robinson, but those wearing the number at that time were permitted to continue to do so. Mo was the last "42" player remaining – just a further testament to his longevity. He will be greatly missed by the Yankee faithful, and by all baseball fans.

The first World Series championship for the "core four" was in 1996. In Game One of that World Series, on a cold New York night, 19-year old Andruw Jones of the Braves stroked two home runs and led Atlanta to a 12-1 victory over Andy Pettitte and the Yankees. That night, Yankee nation, this author included (I was shivering in the Stadium stands that evening watching his power display), hated Andruw Jones.

Jones now plays for the Yankees. Last Sunday afternoon, I and some friends went to watch the Yankees play the Detroit Tigers. In the middle of the eighth inning, the Yankees led by a 5-2 count. Mariano Rivera started taking some warm-up tosses in the bullpen, and prepared to enter the game in the ninth inning to close out the New York victory. But in the bottom of the eighth, Andruw Jones, yes, former Atlanta-wunderkid Andruw Jones, slammed a home run into the seats to give the Yankees a four-run cushion. With the "save opportunity" removed, robo-manager Joe Girardi told Rivera to sit down, and instead sent David Robertson out to pitch the ninth inning and Robertson, presumably the team's new closer, handled the job and the Yankees posted a 6-2 win.

When Jones hit the home run and we saw Robertson get up in the bullpen to throw, I noted my displeasure with Jones' effort, and that because I do not expect to get to too many games this year, it might have been the last chance that I would have to hear the strains of *"Enter Sandman"* as Rivera jogged in from the bullpen. I noted that it might have been my last chance to be in the ballpark to watch number 42 mow down the opposition to seal a Yankees' victory. Earlier in the year Rivera was hinting that this might be his last year; and I was feeling a sense of finality last Sunday.

Little did I know that I may never even see Rivera pitch again, either in person or on television. Little did I know that the home run last Sunday would be more damaging to me than his two 1996 blasts. So I hate Andruw Jones even more now, because he is the man who, with his eighth-inning home run in an otherwise meaningless April game, precluded me from seeing the great Mariano Rivera pitch one last time.

**Extra innings:   My concerns were unwarranted. Mariano is returning for the 2013 season, and has announced that it will be his last. Given the current state of the Yankees' team, it is safe to assume that his number of saves will be down this year, due not to his abilities but due to a lack of opportunities. Assuming that he is able to save 32 games this year, which seems reasonable, he will retire with an all-time record total of 640 regular-season saves. Simple math reveals that any contender to break this record would have to average 40 saves per year for 16 seasons just to tie Mariano. Logic tells us that this will never be accomplished, and that Rivera's all-time saves record, like Cy Young's unassailable record of 511 career victories and Joe DiMaggio's 56-game hitting streak, will live in the record books forever.**

**Apparently any chapter regarding Mariano Rivera has yet to be written, which is a relief, pun intended, to all Yankees' fans, in fact to all baseball fans, who will now be able to experience the thrill of watching number 42 pitch a well-deserved "victory lap" around the major leagues.**

**THE END**

## *ALSO BY ANDREW WOLFENSON*

*"People may hate lawyers but they love to read about them and this book proves why. **In His Own Defense** is a realistic look at the human drama that surrounds a high-stakes criminal case. The pitch-perfect prose and provocative plot compel you to read on, late into the night. New Jersey's own Andy Wolfenson is a north-of-the-Mason-Dixon line answer to John Grisham."* – Henry Kllngeman, Esq., Criminal Defense attorney and former Assistant U.S. Attorney for the State of New Jersey.

**What happens when an attorney is wrongfully accused of murdering a client's husband? Are conversations and interactions between the client and attorney protected by the Attorney-Client privilege, or is the attorney capable of defending himself against the false accusation, even if his actions prove damaging to the client?**

Eric Goldberg is a New Jersey attorney who is first seduced, and then falsely accused of murder, by one of his clients. While testing the boundaries of the attorney-client privilege in conversations with the local police, he travels to Brazil to locate the one person who can clear his name. There, he gains the assistance of a transplanted American architect and his free-spirited, exhibitionist girlfriend, who lead him through the streets and clubs of Sao Paulo searching for his accuser. All the while, American and Brazilian police are searching for him.

*"In His Own Defense" is available on Amazon.com and for Kindle*

184

18407001R00098

Made in the USA
Charleston, SC
01 April 2013